HOUSES in TIME

HOUSES in TIME

A Tour Through New Mexico History

Linda G. Harris

Photography by Pamela Porter

ARROYO PRESS

Las Cruces • New Mexico

Published by
Arroyo Press
P.O. Box 4333, Las Cruces, NM 88003
(505) 522-2348
Printed in Hong Kong.
01 00 99 98 97 5 4 3 2 1

Harris, Linda G.
    Houses in time: a tour through New Mexico history / [text] by
Linda G. Harris; photographs by Pamela Porter
    p. cm.
    Includes bibliographical references and index
    ISBN 1-887045-01-5
    1. New Mexico—History—Pictorial works. 2. Dwellings—
New Mexico—Pictorial works. 3. Architecture, Domestic—New
Mexico—Pictorial works. I. Porter, Pamela. II. Title.
F797.H374 1997
978.9—dc21
                                                        96-38063
                                                          CIP

To

Jim and Christine
and to
Alison

Contents

Preface

This book had its beginnings in December 1993 when I received a sale catalog from the University of Oklahoma Press. For a bargain, I bought a book titled *Oklahoma Homes, Past and Present*. I was born in Oklahoma and was curious to see what the authors could offer about a state whose architectural identity brought to mind oil well derricks. Instead, I found among the 400 captioned photographs, a picture of a rock house like my grandmother's. In another, a two-story frame house reminded me of the story of the night my uncle rescued his cousin from the top of a burning staircase. Houses, I decided, have their own histories.

New Mexico, with its more exotic architectural heritage, is well represented in books about adobe homes. But adobe is only part of the architectural history. I also know from studying my own hometown of Las Cruces that the way people build their homes tells much about their economic and cultural status. I suspected the same would be true for the rest of the state.

I set out to trace New Mexico's history through that most personal of architectural forms, its homes. Following what I call breakable rules, I decided that the book should have geographic breadth and should offer architectural variety. Although nearly every house in the book is still a home, a few are now restaurants or museums; two are historic ruins. The one unbreakable rule was that the book should lead the reader on a tour through New Mexico's history.

Every community in New Mexico has its importance, and every town its favorite old house. No doubt many deserve inclusion in the book. However, the limits of time and the finality of a deadline sometimes made the choice for me.

While many of the homes photographed for the book are registered as historic places, some are merely historically interesting. Regardless, all are studies in local history. As such, I relied not only on published sources, but also on personal interviews, information gleaned from local history museums, city libraries, and the invaluable knowledge of local historians.

Pamela Porter photographed the houses in black and white using available light. Her goal was not to dramatize the homes—for the most part these are simple dwellings—but to underscore their individualities. All of these homes still exist and most can be viewed from the street.

The book is designed to be read all the way through, or simply page by page. Each essay connects a house to its time in history, the first nearly a thousand years ago and last, just yesterday. The aim is to pique your curiosity, to make you wonder why people build their homes as they do. If you also understand and appreciate those reasons, the reward is yours.

Linda G. Harris

Introduction

A house reveals much about its place in time—timber and stone confirm its origin, while gable and window define its era. A house can represent prosperity or poverty. It can show allegiance to tradition, or the influence of outsiders. A single house, like a single chapter, tells but part of New Mexico's history. Only when the houses are collected and bound together, is that history complete.

No other state in the union can lay claim to an architectural heritage as ancient and enduring as New Mexico's. Today's Santa Fe Style houses, the color of earth, of the earth, evolved from ancient cliff dwellings. These apartment-like houses, tucked into sheltering caves, were home to the Anasazi, New Mexico's earliest residents. When their pueblo descendants migrated to the river valleys about a thousand years ago, they lived in adobe homes similar to those of the Anasazi. The nomadic Navajos, who arrived in New Mexico in the late 1400s, built *hogans*, a building tradition they brought with them from the north. However, pueblo architecture persisted, in part because it was native to the landscape, but also because it proved adaptable to city living.

The Spanish contribution to pueblo architecture was one of modification. The Spaniards who colonized New Mexico in 1598 came from a similar arid climate and building tradition. They brought tools for cutting and carving wood, and introduced the use of wooden forms for making adobe bricks. The melding of the Pueblo with the Spanish architectural tradition produced the style that would be uniquely New Mexico's own.

New Mexico's enforced isolation was ended in 1821 during the interlude of Mexican rule when the region was opened to foreign trade, primarily along the Santa Fe Trail. American wagons rolled into Santa Fe laden with goods of a quantity and quality New Mexicans had never before seen. With trade as the opening wedge, the United States easily claimed New Mexico for itself in 1846. Following the Civil War, the army began building permanent forts throughout the territory, in the process creating an architectural style enthusiastically copied for houses in town. The Americans used fired bricks, milled lumber and window glass to put their Territorial imprint on New Mexico's adobe buildings.

Perhaps no event in New Mexico history had a greater effect on its architecture than the coming of the railroad in 1879. The rails crossed the territory in double time, changing the shape and character of old towns and creating new ones nearly overnight. The railroad not only introduced a dizzying variety of house styles, it also brought the materials to build them. In an early expression of corporate identity, the Santa Fe railroad adopted the Mission style for its depots and Harvey Houses. As a result, houses in New Mexico's railroad towns began to sport red-tile roofs.

Architecture in New Mexico's mining towns nearly always meant Victorian, the era that produced the ubiquitous Queen Anne and the occasional Italianate. As with most of the styles that reached New Mexico, Victorian arrived a little out of fashion. Nevertheless, mining towns produced many a fine Victorian that would regain its glory in another time.

The Homestead Act of 1862 and the opportunity of the open range populated New Mexico's farms and ranches with men and women of hardy ambition. When they could, they built houses in the style of their hometowns. If not, they simply accepted what New Mexico offered, added their own touches, and got on with their business.

About the time of statehood, a group of artists and writers formed art colonies in Taos and Santa Fe. They lived cheaply in old adobes, and studied New Mexico's native culture first-hand. From their cultural immersion blossomed not only painting and poetry, but also an advocacy for New Mexico's cultural preservation, particularly its architectural heritage.

New Mexico in the half-century following World War II faced greater changes than in any other period of its history. Wartime defense installations were converted into Cold War research laboratories and testing ranges, creating jobs for an eager post-war population. Builders met the pent-up demand for housing by creating entire neighborhoods from mesquite covered sand hills. While Albuquerque, and to a lesser extent Las Cruces, prospered from the science and defense industries, Santa Fe reaped its own rewards as the tourist destination of the trendy.

Progress, however, became the downfall of New Mexico's old neighborhoods and downtown districts. Beginning in the 1960s adobe and Victorian houses fell victim to the demand for more modern houses, while main street stores suffered under the competition from shopping centers. Efforts at urban renewal only made things worse. Out of the lessons of urban renewal, however, dawned the historic preservation movement. Neighborhood associations have reclaimed their old communities, restoring and living in once-neglected Victorians. Main Street America projects have helped cities restore economic and social life in their downtowns. Cities have documented the architectural and historical lives of their old houses and buildings in published surveys.

Perhaps New Mexico's greatest hope for historic preservation lies in its houses. As structures of living history, houses survive only so long as people—regardless of their place in history or society—make them their homes. In the end, houses remain the touchstones of our histories, our placeholders in time.

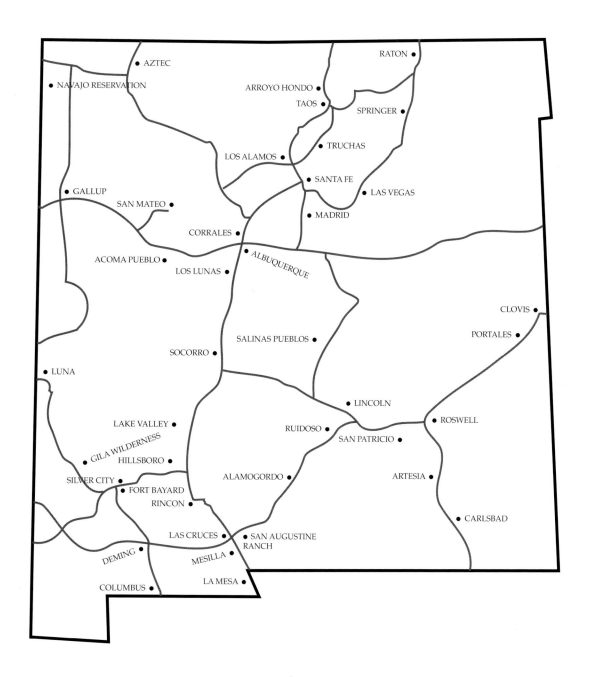

Acoma Houses

Acoma Pueblo
Circa 1200

Cloud wisps float above Acoma Pueblo like a magician's scarves suspended in thin air. In the distance, jet contrails scrawl a modern signature across the chill December sky. The pueblo, built on the sandstone mesa some 400 feet above the valley floor, is quiet but for the muted chatter of a small party of tourists. They have come to see what is said to be the oldest continuously occupied city in the United States.

Nearly a thousand years ago, around 1200, legend has it that Iatiku, "mother of all Indians" guided a Keresan-speaking people to Acoma. They believed *Acoma*, meaning "a place of preparedness," to be the center of the earth. Iatiku instructed them to build houses, gathering together rocks and sticks and dirt herself for the job. Soon they had a town, laid out according to her plan, with houses of mud and stone standing shoulder to shoulder facing the direction of the warm winter sun. Flat-roofed and rectangular, the houses set the architectural style that would survive to become the nation's oldest architectural tradition.

Predating Iatiku's architectural revelation by some 400 years, however, were the emerging house building techniques of the Anasazi Culture, the ancestors to the Acoma. By 700 the Anasazi had given up their nomadic ways of hunters and gatherers for the fairly settled lives of farmers. Soon they had traded their primitive pithouses for above-ground flat-roofed homes built of poles and mud. Later, the Anasazi built improved "apartments" of stone and adobe, setting them side-by-side like dominoes, stacking some units two and three stories high. Sixteenth-century Spanish explorers gave these settlements the designation *pueblo*, which means town in Spanish.

By the time Spanish explorers began to traverse the region, Acoma Pueblo was a well-known landmark. Fray Marcos, in deliberate overstatement, described it as a "kingdom," while one of Coronado's men called Acoma "the greatest stronghold ever seen in the world." When Juan de Oñate, New Mexico's colonizer and its first governor, reached Acoma Pueblo in the fall of 1598, he reported the high fortress as having 500 apartments. The only access, for inhabitant and outsider alike, he observed, was by handholds and toeholds hollowed from its sandstone cliffs.

Before winter was out, Oñate's fate as governor and his place in history would be determined by the massacre at Acoma. When a small party of Oñate's men stopped at the pueblo for food and supplies, the Indians ambushed them, killing 13. Oñate retaliated in a three-day battle, killing 600 to 800 Acomas and burning the pueblo to the ground. Oñate was eventually charged with crimes of colonial mismanagement, including the massacre at Acoma, for which he was fined and condemned to perpetual exile from New Mexico. Within a couple of years, the Acomas reoccupied the mesa and rebuilt the pueblo.

Four hundred years later, tourists follow their soft-spoken guide past adobe beehive ovens, called *hornos* (in foreground). During feast days, Acoma women will fire the ovens to bake the celebratory bread in the way of their mothers and their ancient mothers before them.

Gila Cliff Dwellings

Gila Wildnerness
Circa 1270

Each day for centuries the early morning sun has angled its way into the dark alcoves of Cliff Dweller Canyon, illuminating the ancient apartments with its buttery light. At first the sandstone dwellings look nearly molten, about to overflow at the edges. But when the sun leaves them in shadow, they spend the rest of the day in silvery blue light.

In about 1270, for only one generation, prehistoric Indians lived in these shaded niches. These were the people of the Mogollon culture, one of three related cultures to inhabit the desert Southwest during ancient times. The three—the Mogollon, the Hohokam of southern Arizona, and the Anasazi of the Four Corners region—traded goods, and shared ideas and home-building techniques.

Archaeologists believe that about 10,000 years ago New Mexico's earliest inhabitants lived at least part-time in the caves of Cliff Dweller Canyon. The cliffs themselves are three to six million years old. The Mogollon, however, first settled the valley below in pithouse villages where they tended small plots of corn, beans and squash. Later they lived in rectangular houses with T-shaped doorways, much like those of their Anasazi neighbors to the north.

The Anasazi also influenced Mogollon pottery techniques and design. But about a thousand years ago in the period known as the Mimbres Phase of their culture, the Mogollon developed a distinctive pottery style that today defines their legacy. In unparalleled craftsmanship, they created pottery with intricate black-on-white depictions of birds, bears, rabbits and fish. More importantly, their drawings pictured the daily lives of their own people.

By the time the Gila Cliff Dwellings were built, the Mogollon culture was on the wane. The caves provided shelter and safety, but in the farming terraces below, water was becoming increasingly scarce. By the 1300s when the Mogollon abandoned the cliff dwellings, they had nearly lost their cultural identity. Some archaeologists speculate that they scattered to the pueblo villages in northern Arizona and New Mexico and along the Rio Grande Valley.

For the next six hundred years, the ancient apartments sat abandoned, sheltered in the cliff's sandstone hollows. Not until the late 1800s did the first white man report on the dwellings, the news of which soon attracted souvenir-hunting cowboys. Teddy Roosevelt, who as a young man had found solace in the West, turned his reformer's attention westward when he became president. In 1907 President Roosevelt created the Gila Cliff Dwellings National Monument, which today lies protected in the midst of the 558,000-acre Gila National Wilderness.

Gran Quivera

Salinas Pueblos
Circa 1600

When the last of the Mogollon abandoned their pueblo in about 1300, some of their people migrated to Gran Quivera at the hard edge of pueblo civilization. Gran Quivera, one of the Salinas Pueblos, occupied a windy mesa overlooking the crusty remains of an ancient shallow sea. Here the Mogollon became the newest residents in a city that had only recently given up its pithouses for more modern communal apartments. The apartments, some 200 rooms laid out in five or six concentric circles, were built of sandstone blocks cemented with yellow caliche mortar.

By the 1500s Gran Quivera had become a rectangular city with its updated apartments covering over the old circular structures. (The ruins shown here date from the 1600s.) The unlikely outpost also had become an important trading center for Anasazi and Apache alike. Over time Gran Quivera had made the most of its status as a commercial crossroads and its proximity to the saline lake beds 24 miles away. Gran Quivera's population often doubled to more than 3,000 as Pueblo and Plains Indians congregated at the pueblo for trade fairs. The mesa-top hummed with the mixed dialects of Indian, and later, Spanish, traders. Hunters likely offered dried bison and pronghorn meat in trade for black-and-white Tibrá pots, cotton blankets, or turquoise and shell jewelry. Salt from the saline lakes, packed in leather pouches, was a favorite trading commodity among the Indians. When the Spanish colonizer Juan de Oñate visited the pueblo in 1598 he reported that the Indians "eat it alone, or suck it just as we do sugar." Oñate, however, viewed the salt deposits from a miner's perspective. Salt, Oñate knew, was a key ingredient in smelting silver. Oñate's father had made his fortune in the silver mines in Zacatecas, Mexico, a feat Oñate hoped to repeat in New Mexico.

Although Oñate failed to find his silver in New Mexico, a rich strike at Parral, Mexico, in 1631 provided a ready market for salt. Spanish caravans began carrying loads of bagged salt as well as captured Apaches to the silver mine at Parral. To add to their woes, the marginal lands of the Salinas Pueblos, including those of Gran Quivera, could no longer support the population. Rainfall, always scarce, came less and less and hunting grounds became depleted. The now desperate Apaches turned from trading with the Pueblos to raiding their villages. Disease took its toll. By the time of the Pueblo Revolt against the Spanish in 1680, Gran Quivera was already deserted.

Luna Jacál

Lincoln
Circa 1868

Jacales were the first aboveground homes of the early Anasazi who lived in the Four Corners region more than a thousand years ago. They built these lightweight homes of vertical poles which were set into the ground, woven together with brush, and plastered inside and out with adobe mud. *Jacales* were tiny places, usually 6 to 14 feet across, their size dictated by the length of the roof timbers. The flat roofs also were covered with a layer of twigs and plastered with *adobe*.

By the time the Spanish colonists arrived in the 1600s, Spanish Pueblo had become the building style of choice. The *jacál*, however, still found practical use as a storage building as well as an animal shelter. The colonists, equipped with metal tools, were able to cut larger logs for both the sidewalls and the roof, thus extending the room size to about 15 feet. In southern New Mexico where timber was less plentiful and the climate drier, *jacales* often were simple unplastered brush huts. *Jacál* construction remained much in evidence until the late 1800s.

The *jacál* pictured here is located next to a house built by Ramón Luna sometime around 1868. Over time, the *jacál* served as both home and storage building for the Luna family. The Lincoln County Heritage Trust has restored the one-room *jacál* to represent the typical home of Lincoln's early Hispanic settlers. The 9 feet by 16 feet dwelling is homey with its whitewashed walls, packed dirt floor and corner fireplace. So homey, in fact, that during the 1920s Mr. and Mrs. Solomon Luna lived in the *jacál* as newlyweds.

Hogan

Navajo Reservation, New Mexico

West of Shiprock the setting sun glints on an old Navajo woman dressed in a velvet blouse belted over a full "Navajo" skirt. She walks easily up a slight incline toward her house and *hogan*. Further on ponies graze in perfect pose near the highway. As Highway 64 nears Farmington twilight gives way to a lively convergence of headlights and tail lights. This is *Dinétah*—Navajo Country—where Navajo culture remains as traditional as its *hogans* and as dynamic as traffic on a Friday night.

The 17.5 million-acre Navajo Reservation stretches north from New Mexico into Utah and west into Arizona. Just over a quarter of its 200,000 population live in New Mexico, making it by far the state's most populous Indian reservation. While they struggle to sustain a viable economy, the Navajo have fared amazingly well considering their recent entry into New Mexico Native American history.

The Navajo were latecomers to the Native American Southwest, migrating here from the north sometime in the 1400s. The Navajo in prehistoric times had been hunters, gatherers and fishermen. In the Southwest, however, they adopted some of the farming techniques— as well as the ceremonial lore—of their Pueblo neighbors. The Navajo later preferred raising livestock, particularly horses, sheep and goats, which the Spaniards had introduced when they colonized New Mexico in 1598. Although some Navajos lived in pueblo villages, they found homesteads better suited to a livelihood devoted mainly to herding. On the homesteads they lived in *hogans* similar to the Navajo dwelling Fray Alonso de Benavides described in 1603 as an "earth-covered dwelling."

Until recently, the *hogan*—which means "home place" or "dwelling area"—was not only the family home but also a place where the traditions and religious lessons of Navajo life were taught. Today, the *hogan* more likely sits next to a modern home and is used either for ceremonial practices or for storage. Many families have two *hogans*, one for each purpose. Navajo *hogans* are built in many variations on a theme. However, they usually are multi-sided with a conical shaped roof. The single door always faces toward the sunrise. They are usually windowless and have a smoke hole in the roof directly above a hearth. Most have dirt floors, although concrete is used in some recent styles. *Hogans* today can be constructed of brush, logs, stone, earth, or even artificial siding.

The *hogan* shown here is constructed with rock and cribbed-logs, covered entirely in earth. Earth-covered *hogans* are particularly suited to the Southwest where soil and stone are the only abundant sources of building materials and where the climate is dry. Some archaeologists believe the earth-covering is a technique borrowed from Pueblo builders. Basic cribbed-log construction, however, is a traditional Navajo building technique. In this method, logs are placed in alternating tiers with the number of logs decreasing in each tier until they converge to form the roof. The result is a *hogan* with fairly straight walls ending in a beehive-shaped roof.

Oldest House

215 East DeVargas Street, Santa Fe
Circa 1740

Whether the long *adobe* stretching along DeVargas Street is the "oldest house" in the continental United States or even the "oldest house" in Santa Fe, has long been a source of speculation. Archaeologists know that beginning about 600, ancestors of the modern Pueblo Indians lived along the Santa Fe River, but abandoned their riverside village in about 1425. During the 1880s, Adolph Bandelier, the father of Southwestern archeology, studied a number of prehistoic pueblos in Santa Fe County and speculated that fifteenth-century ruins of a Tano-speaking village in Santa Fe lay buried in the vicinity of San Miguel Church. The "oldest house" is located across from the church on DeVargas Street on original church property. Records of San Miguel Church date back to 1626 when Fray Alonso de Benavides reported the chapel was already in use as a parish church.

Edgar Hewett, then director of the School of American Archaeology, in a 1910 article for the *Santa Fe New Mexican*, seemed to confirm Bandelier's view when he suggested that one of three pueblo ruins lay near San Miguel Church and the "oldest house."

The historian Ralph Emerson Twitchell disputed Hewett's premise, writing also in the *New Mexican*, that no such pueblo existed in the vicinity of San Miguel Church. He conceded, however, that the "oldest house" was probably of pueblo construction.

A José Urrutia map of the city drawn up in 1766-1768 shows a building in the approximate location of the house. Tree-ring specimens taken from the *vigas* in the first-floor ceilings date the house from 1740-1767. By the time the J.J. Stoner map was drawn up in 1882, the house had received the designation as the "oldest building" in Santa Fe.

Today the old building has been smoothed and made presentable to the thousands of tourists who visit Santa Fe each year. A restaurant at one end of the house serves pizza. Next to the cash register, however, is a low door leading to rooms that retain the rough, dark features of an earlier time. Low ceilings, a dirt floor and walls heavy with thick *adobe* offer a glimpse of life in Santa Fe from who knows how many centuries ago.

Ortega House

Highway 76, Truchas
Circa 1753

The air is mountaintop crisp as Pedro Ribera Ortega rounds the corner of the rambling adobe to face the morning sun. He wears a black, flat brimmed hat, several shirts and a black wool coat buttoned to the chin. His garb, like his house, is layered for warmth.

Ortega, looking the part of an old Spaniard, is a retired school teacher and fervent historian who relates in storyteller fashion the history of his house. He believes part of the house may have formed one corner of a fortress village dating from the founding of Truchas in 1753 when a dozen families received Spanish land grants totaling 10,000 acres. In exchange, their settlement was to serve as a buffer to prevent Comanches from raiding villages in the Española and Mora valleys below.

Their willingness to put themselves in harm's way for the promise of free land typifies both hope and desperation in eighteenth-century New Mexico colonists. Spain nearly abandoned its colonial outpost early on when its quest for riches yielded only hardship. Instead, the Spaniards stayed on to exploit the Indians' labor and to put the Catholic stamp on their souls. In 1680 the Pueblo Indians revolted, killing 400 Spaniards and driving the rest out of New Mexico. Even after the Reconquest in 1693, the province remained a neglected corner of the Spanish empire. For the founders of Truchas,

the only recourse was to look after themselves. For good measure, they chose not one but three patron saints to protect their fortress village—Nuestra Señora del Rosario La Conquistadora, San Fernando Rey, and Santiago.

The Ortega house seems as richly blessed. It has sixteen rooms, their outside walls of thick adobe. A portion of a kitchen wall, however, exposes the thick upright posts of *jacál* construction, which was used for the interior walls. The ceiling logs are "Truchas *vigas*," the squared, hand-hewn roof beams introduced by the Spanish. Ortega also points out that the heavy timbers that support the bookcases were salvaged from a log cabin. The walls in nearly every room on the lower floor are covered with books—35,000 by the historian's count.

Back outside, the sun shines full on the tin roof, the architectural marker that identifies the house as New Mexico Vernacular, or Northern New Mexico style. The pitched roof helps shed the winter snows that frequent these altitudes. Fall, however, is just days old, and amaranth still blooms across the front of the house. In times past, Spanish women used its reddish purple leaves to rouge their cheeks, Ortega explains. "It's called the happiness plant."

Martínez Hacienda

Ranchitos Road, Taos
Circa 1824

If New Mexico's architectural identity was born of the Pueblo culture, its character was formed by Spanish colonists. These Spaniards were heirs to an architectural tradition—based on aridity and borrowed from the Moors—which was surprisingly similar to that of the Pueblos. The Spanish, however, possessed the knowledge and the tools that both improved and refined Pueblo construction. The most important modification was in adobe making. The Indians made their homes of "coursed," *adobe* using a long, laborious process in which adobe mud was compacted and laid in courses to form walls about two feet thick. Each layer had to dry before the next course was added. The Spaniards instead mass-produced *adobe* bricks. The *adobe* mixture (clay, sand, water and sometimes straw) was packed into wooden forms which were then lifted off allowing the bricks to dry in a day or two. The thicker, stronger bricks supported larger structures. In addition, the Spaniards laid the *adobes* on a stone foundation, which prevented erosion at the ground level.

The Martinez Hacienda illustrates many of the architectural characteristics of the Spanish Pueblo style. In 1804 Don Antonio Severino Martinez bought a four-room building situated on the banks of the Rio Pueblo. The successful businessman and politician expanded the building into a *hacienda*, which would serve both as trading headquarters and fortress. The *hacienda*, which has been restored as a museum, consists of 21 rooms arranged single file around two *placitas*, or small interior plazas.

The *hacienda* exterior (right) shows the sculpted massing of the *adobe* walls and supporting buttress. The windowless outside walls protected the hacienda from attack and from the weather. The only entry was through a *zaguán* gate, which was wide enough to admit livestock and *carretas*, or carts such as the one shown here. A *canale* was used to drain rainwater from the flat roof. The roof's parapet, or upper extension, provided a lookout and when needed, a gunpost.

The "shepherd's bed" in the kitchen (opposite) made a handy bunk next to the fireplace. The *placita* well seen through the door ensured a convenient and protected source of water in times of siege.

Casa de Armijo

308 San Felipe NW, Albuquerque
Circa 1840

Albuquerque's founding in 1706 was simply a matter of business. The provisional governor believed that Albuquerque's rich river valley lands would benefit farmers and that its location along the trade route between Santa Fe and Mexico would profit merchants. Although the governor neglected to request official permission for Albuquerque's founding until after the fact, his business sense proved correct.

At first the settlers, mostly Spaniards, *mestizos* and *mulattoes*, lived on farms scattered along the valley. This settlement pattern was more convenient for the farmers, but it also left them vulnerable to Indian raids. For the first 75 years, Albuquerque itself consisted mainly of the church and a few "Sunday houses" built around the plaza. The villa of Albuquerque eventually grew to become a full-time settlement where craftspeople, farmers and traders lived and worked.

By the late 1820s, Ambrosio Armijo, a descendant of one of the founding families of New Mexico and brother of Governor Manuel Armijo, had become a prosperous Albuquerque merchant and Santa Fe trader. From his headquarters on the plaza, he also operated a thriving import business. Sometime around 1872—the exact date is unknown—one of his imports was a walnut staircase from Spain. He installed it in his home on the east side of the plaza as the centerpiece for his daughter Teresa's wedding. When the lovely Teresa descended the stair on her wedding day, a train of satin and lace trailed 30 feet behind, the exact length of the staircase.

Today, diners can take the bride's stairway to visit a small art gallery while they wait for tables at La Placita Dining Rooms, the restaurant that now occupies the first floor of the Casa de Armijo.

Gurule House

133 Martinez, Santa Fe
Circa 1930

You know you're in New Mexico when directions to an old schoolhouse include "go three miles past the brown house with the Virgin of Guadalupe in the front yard." In New Mexico, it's not uncommon to find a shrine in the front yard, a saint tucked into a living room *nicho*, or a collection of Virgin Marys lined up to view the passing traffic.

New Mexico's affection for its communion of saints dates to the conquest of Mexico. When Hernán Cortés landed on the coast of Mexico in 1519, he brought sacred images ashore to illustrate the power of the one Christian God. In 1598, ten Franciscan friars accompanied Oñate on his colonizing expedition into New Mexico. He established the colonial capital at San Juan (near present-day Española) in July of that year. Within a month the friars had erected New Mexico's first church, naming St. John the Baptist as its patron saint.

By 1631 the Franciscans had established 34 Indian missions in New Mexico. In their efforts to Christianize the Indians, the friars also set up mission schools where they taught the Indians to read, write, and carve wood. The next fifty years, however, found the church at odds with their civil counterparts over rights to exploit Indian labor. It is not surprising then that in the Pueblo Revolt of 1680, the Indians burned both church and *hacienda*.

By the 1700s, Spain had left the colonists and the church more or less to their own devices. As a result, life in New Mexico continued its distinctive religious and cultural evolution, unbothered and unaided by distant authorities. That meant local villages had to create the religious images, or *santos*, for their own churches, and later their homes. They used common materials such as pine boards or buffalo hide as canvas for their paintings, called *retablos*. Woodcarvers turned cottonwood and pine saplings into the elongated bodies of saints, carvings in the round called *bultos*. Ironically, the Franciscans had focused on teaching the Indians useful crafts, while neglecting to teach these arts to the Spanish peasants. In the end, the peasant became the self-taught *santero*, the maker of sacred images, while New Mexico's Indians showed no interest in that folk art at all. Since then, *santo*-making has become a respected craft with some *santeros* gaining individual acclaim for their art.

Emma Gurule's ceramic and carved religious figures fill the front window of the family home in Santa Fe (opposite). Mrs. Gurule, who was both a Catholic and a lover of dolls, for 25 years collected figures of Christ, the Virgin Mary and an assembly of saints. The easygoing expression of her faith is a reminder for all who pass by of the historical alliance between religion and culture in New Mexico.

Kit Carson House

Kit Carson Road, Taos

1825

The legendary Kit Carson might be surprised to find that today the most tangible symbol of his fame as a fur-trapper and Indian fighter is his house. The 12-room house dates from 1825, but Carson bought it in 1843 as a wedding gift for his young bride, Josefa Jaramillo. Theirs was a fortunate match. Carson was famous in his own right, and Josefa was from a prominent Taos family. Her sister also married well, to Governor Charles Bent. Bent, however, was murdered in the Indian revolt of 1847.

The kitchen, one of the house's three restored rooms, provides a somewhat sterile look at the domestic life of a prosperous New Mexico family in the mid-1800s. Back then, the kitchen would have been full of lively conversation and the aroma of spicy corn stew simmering in a kettle. Trails of piñon smoke would have blackened the corner fireplace, which was called a *fogón de campana* for its bellshaped hood. Its double hearths, unusual even to that time, were the sign of Carson's large household—he and Josefa eventually would have eight children.

Barela de Bledsoe House

7017 Edith NE, Albuquerque
Circa 1840

When Mexico gained its independence from Spain in 1821, New Mexico came under the benign rule of its new government. History books give the Mexican colonial period (a scant 25 years) only parenthetical mention in the larger discussions of Spanish colonial New Mexico. What Mexico did do, however, was open trade with the United States. Under Spanish rule, New Mexico's borders had been sealed to outside trade, leaving it the economic option of trading only with Mexico City by way of the official government trade route, *El Camino Real*. For more than 200 years economic protectionism kept New Mexico both dependent upon and impoverished by the Spanish colonial government.

Within a year of Mexico's nineteenth-century trade initiative, new economic forces had begun the slow reshaping of New Mexico. Its houses, reflecting these influences, took on subtle changes for the first time in more than two centuries. The 1840s Barela de Bledsoe house, for example, had been built in the security-minded fashion of the Spanish Pueblo style. Its windowless fortress-like walls were squared up to form a protective *placita*. *Vigas* extended from the parapet of its flat roof. Before long, however, windows were cut into the solid walls (opposite) and dressed for company in a new architectural style. The Americans were coming.

Territorial Door

1305 South Pacific Street, Las Vegas
Circa 1870

This weathered old door on South Pacific Street seems to be taking a siesta. Do not disturb. The threshold steps, however, are an inviting perch for afternoon daydreaming. What would South Pacific Street have been like in 1870, when the steps were sturdy and newly painted? Dusty, for one thing. Back then the street was a thoroughfare for ox carts and covered wagons leaving the Las Vegas plaza for their final destination in Santa Fe. The founders of Las Vegas had the foresight in 1835 to establish the town astride the Santa Fe Trail, the trade route linking Independence, Missouri, to Santa Fe, 800 miles away. Seventy-five wagons rolled into Las Vegas the very first year, and by 1870 the town was well established as New Mexico's port of entry. From the plaza markets, caravans replenished their supplies of fresh vegetables, fruits and cheeses. In turn, plaza merchants traded for imported goods ranging from ribbons to knives to padlocks.

American imports had begun to transform New Mexicans into Americans even before the U.S. Army made it official in 1846. When this house was built in 1870, it was surprising that it was fashioned after a style so popular back East that the Americans dubbed it the "National Style." When the style, later renamed Greek Revival, reached New Mexico after the Civil War, it arrived pared to its simplest form—an elegant complement to the earthy *adobe*. Architects would later designate this New Mexico version of Greek Revival with yet a third name, Territorial style.

The door shown here has two elements crucial to the Territorial style—glass and milled lumber. Thanks to the Santa Fe traders, window glass was available in New Mexico for the first time, while sawmills were introduced courtesy of the U.S. Army. Civilians admired, then adopted, the military's Greek Revival style of construction that overlaid the traditional adobe with porches, windows and doors made of sawn lumber and painted bright white. Glass transom and sidelight windows are as recognizable here in their Greek Revival form as they would be fronting a Mississippi mansion. The pilasters of the door frame are simple renditions of the classic pillars of the Parthenon. The door itself is a factory-made Victorian, no doubt added after the turn of the century when Territorial's popularity had begun to wane.

Romero House

1409 South Pacific Street, Las Vegas
Circa 1879

In 1851 Miguel Romero began his mercantile career as a wagon master on the Santa Fe Trail, freighting goods from Las Vegas to St. Louis. His business became so successful that in 1878 he founded the Romero Mercantile Company, a dry goods store that occupied a choice spot on the plaza in Las Vegas. There he and his five sons built the business into the Southwest's leading wholesale dry goods distributor. The brothers also shared an interest in Republican politics, land grant issues, and charitable causes. Eugenio, for example, helped organize the New Mexico Brass Band.

The Romero *familia* had no trouble filling up the fourteen rooms of the massive adobe referred to as the *Casa Redonda*, or round house. The house actually *surrounds* a central *placita*, or courtyard. Later the house served as the Jesuit School for Boys, and from 1875 to 1919 was the headquarters for *La Revisita Catolica*, the leading Spanish-language Jesuit newspaper. Today *Casa Redonda* is back in use as a home to multiple families. Note the Territorial door trim above the courtyard entrance.The small closely spaced blocks that fill the pedimented lintel gives it a gap-toothed look. The blocks are called dentils, as in dentures.

Benigno Romero House

2003 Hot Springs Boulevard, Las Vegas

1874

The Santa Fe trade created a class of merchants in Las Vegas whose fine homes were in keeping with their wealth and influence. Merchants with names like Baca, Ilfeld, and Romero one day would be remembered as much for their homes as for their accomplishments. Of them all, however, the Benigno Romero house tells as much about the man as it does his house-building.

Benigno Romero, one of Miguel Romero's prosperous sons, built this two-story *adobe* just north of the plaza where he could keep an eye on his many enterprises. His was the era's ideal "mansion." In a departure from the traditional one-story *adobe*, Romero built his two stories high and belted it across the middle with a cantilevered balcony. The windows, doors and pitched tin roof follow the Territorial style.

In 1881 Romero formed the Plaza Hotel and Improvement Co., which built the Plaza Hotel, the finest in the Territory. A decade later he founded the Romero Drug Co., where in addition to engaging in the wholesale drug trade, he sold his specially developed patent medicine called *La Sanadora*. During this same period, Romero waged a long campaign for the construction of a hospital for the insane. In those days, the insane either wandered the streets or were jailed. Romero often cared for these unfortunates in his own home. In 1889, the legislature authorized construction of the Territorial Insane Asylum at Las Vegas. The New Mexico State Hospital, as it is now called, is Las Vegas' second largest employer. Today, in small tribute to the man and his house, Benigno Romero's name is lettered on the little rooftop dormer of his "mansion."

Silva House

225 Moreno Street, Las Vegas
Circa 1880

Vicente Silva didn't live in this house because he appreciated its elegance. The murderous gangster lived here, so legend says, because an escape tunnel led from its basement to the river. Although Silva gave the house its dark legacy, credit for its Italian Renaissance facade belongs to the Italian architect Andrea Palladio. In the late 1500s Palladio's country villas were all the rage of Italy's landed gentry. His architectural designs were stripped of pretentious—and expensive—details, relying instead upon proportion and composition for effect. The Palladian window, narrow and topped with a fanlight, became his architectural signature. The restrained symmetry of Palladio's designs appealed to the colonists (American not Spanish) who adopted the style for their New England mansions.

The Silva house is a unique style known as New Mexican Folk Italian Renaissance—"New Mexican Folk" because adobe underlies its red and tan sandstone facade. The arched windows also are uncharacteristic of early New Mexico architecture as New Mexico's native builders never developed the skill to create an arch. Although the building's architect is unknown, Andrea Palladio undoubtedly would be pleased to take the bow.

Pinckney Tully House

136 Grant Avenue, Santa Fe
1851

The Pinckney Tully House would be pure Territorial, but for one touch—its bricks. Bricks are in fact a key element in Territorial design, but normally that means "real" bricks. These are fake, forged by an expert with a sure hand and a true eye. In a remodeling effort worthy of Michelangelo, sometime before 1890, the artisan painted "bricks" directly onto the adobe walls. Five rows of "real" kiln-baked bricks cap the roof line to imitate a Greek dentiled cornice. The middle row is laid with the alternate bricks protruding like jack o'lantern teeth. More commonly, the bricks are set at a forty-five-degree angle. The brick coping not only adds a finishing touch to the roof line, it also protects the *adobe* from erosion.

Although New Mexico's first brick building was constructed in Mesilla in 1863, bricks were still a rare building material. By the 1880s military posts such as Fort Union near Las Vegas and Fort Marcy at Santa Fe had built kilns to fire their own bricks. Silver City, Las Vegas, Santa Fe and Albuquerque also had their own brick plants. By then, brick chimneys sprouted from the more "modern" houses of the day.

About the time the Pinckney Tully house was "bricked," the owners also added a bay window, the first in Santa Fe. By then, however, Pinckney R. Tully was long gone. Within four years of building the nine-room house, Tully, a merchant and trader, had left Santa Fe to establish freighting businesses in Mesilla, New Mexico, and later Tucson, Arizona. Despite a long list of subsequent owners and the bit of remodeling, Mr. Tully today still would recognize his fine Territorial house, even with its new "bricks."

Hinojos House

355 East Palace Avenue, Santa Fe
Late 1800s

Archbishop Jean Baptist Lamy arrived in Santa Fe in 1853 with a zealot's determination and a Frenchman's sensibility. The French priest had just been named New Mexico's first resident bishop. Through his eyes, the diocese was in dire need of sprucing up. Santa Fe's five churches were, he lamented, no better than "the stable of Bethlehem." Its mud houses afforded only a window or two. In the whole of Santa Fe, Lamy saw but one peaked roof. Although Lamy held small hope for reforming domestic architecture, his true dream lay in rebuilding New Mexico's *adobe* churches into stone reminders of Romanesque French cathedrals. He began with the rebuilding of St. Francis Cathedral in Santa Fe.

During construction, Lamy brought in itinerant French artisans from Louisiana to work on the cathedral. These craftsmen often sidelined by building homes for Santa Fe's wealthy residents. Their stylistic influence is evident here in the Doña Francisca Hinojos house where the design hints of Louisiana's French Colonial period. In concession to New Mexico tradition, they built the house of *adobe*. Don Alfredo Hinojos, a prominent politician, inherited the property from his mother in 1887. For nearly fifty years, Don Alfredo also was the cathedral's organist.

Although Lamy died in 1888 with his great cathedral unfinished, the forty-five French-styled churches he built during his tenure had changed architectural skylines throughout his diocese. However, he was never able to work the same conversion on the homes of his parishioners. They ignored the heavy-handed Romanesque as well as the lighter French colonial style of his artisans. Instead they favored a catalog of new styles—Queen Anne, Italianate and California Mission—introduced with the coming of the railroad.

Barela/Taylor House

Calle Principal, Mesilla
1854

Every one of the thirteen rooms in the Barela/Taylor House is filled floor to ceiling with the keepsakes of history—carved folk art saints, large-as-life portraits, handmade quilts, even a ceiling made from rescued *vigas*. But nowhere are the mementos more telling than in the *oratorio*, the family chapel. An eighteenth-century New Mexican *Cristo* hangs above the altar, while the altar itself is draped in cloth embroidered by the Sisters of the Good Shepherd. An antique Mexican confessional is tucked behind the adobe buttress at right. There the gold-embroidered vestments of Father Jean Grange are carefully laid out as if anticipating his return. Father Grange was the parish priest of San Albino Catholic Church just across the plaza. Grange acquired the house in 1917, and used part of the house as a rectory and the adjoining storefront rooms for catechism classes. His was neither the first nor last instance where the Catholic church played a part it the history of the house.

Mesilla was officially founded in 1850, although by then some 3,000 people already were living in the town. By the late 1850s Mesilla was the county seat and southern New Mexico's most prosperous commercial center. The house Rafaela Barela had built in 1854 was home to the first of a succession of merchant families who operated shops on the plaza's west side. Then as now, a narrow passageway led from the plaza to the living quarters behind the shops.

Nearly a century later, new owners explored the house with the curiosity of historians. As Paul and Mary Taylor sorted through the collected debris, they came across a box of papers dating from Father Grange's tenure in the house. These were the journal articles of Bishop Henry Granjon, one of Archbishop Lamy's French priests. In the papers, published in their original French, Granjon had chronicled his 1902 visit to Southwest New Mexico.

Although the Taylors were both historians, they had seven children to raise and a house to restore, so they put the papers aside. Then in 1980 a friend of the Taylors, Mary W. De López, translated the narrative into English, while their son Michael Taylor, also a historian, annotated the journal and wrote the introduction. The resulting book, *Along the Rio Grande*, published in 1988, faithfully preserves Granjon's journal in narrative that is witty, perceptive and graceful. Of Mesilla, he writes, "This is Spain once more, the rural Spain of old, somewhat mixed with Anglo-Saxonism and a relic of Aztec survival."

Reynolds/Chavez/Fountain House

Calle del Picacho, Mesilla
Circa 1860s

The dappled light of early morning feathers the rough edges of the rock fence to water color softness. A desert willow tipped with delicate orchid-like blooms lends pale greens and lavender to the foreground. Just out of sight, water the color of the earth burbles to itself as it drags along the irrigation ditch. It is a perfect setting for a perfect Territorial.

Joseph Reynolds was at the height of his career when he built this house just west of Mesilla's plaza. Reynolds, an Irish immigrant who had come west as a clerk with the U.S. Army, operated a successful mercantile store on the plaza. His *adobe* home followed the symmetrical floor plan typical of Territorial style. What was not typical was its elegance and size. Large rooms, including a music room and game room, led from a grand center hall. In an era when most floors were of packed dirt, Reynolds' were polished hardwood.

When Reynolds died in 1883, Demetrio Chavez, a trusted employee who had managed Reynolds' store, bought both the business and the house. His daughter Maria Chavez and her husband Albert J. Fountain (grandson of the legendary Col. Albert Fountain) raised their family in the house. After the deaths of Albert and Maria, the house sat vacant until it was near ruin. During one attempt at restoration, the owner died before finishing the work. The property was vacant once again. Finally, in 1987 new owners completed the job, restoring the home to its nineteenth-century elegance.

Sanchez House

1195 Mesquite Street, Las Cruces
Late 1800s

In Las Cruces when people talk about the old neighborhood, they mean the *old* neighborhood, the few streets in the original townsite called the Mesquite District. Here in 1849 the first residents built plain-faced adobe houses and set them close to the street. They were walled at the back, not only for protection but also to keep their goats and chickens corralled.

When the two-room Sanchez house was built in the late 1800s, its facade was simple and solid, with its doorway set at a 45-degree angle. In 1928 the building got a facelift of sorts when Carlos and Rosinda Sanchez decided to operate a Mom and Pop grocery store in the house. By then their family numbered eleven children and the house, seventeen rooms. They gave the outside of the building a vaguely Art Deco look by adding a cantilevered awning with rounded pilasters above. Art Deco, a style in vogue about the time of the renovation, was a favorite for commercial buildings. With a combination of creativity and whimsy, the Sanchez couple installed a hand-painted wooden Indian out front to greet customers, and had an artist paint the rising sun over the door to cheer passersby.

Inside, they emptied their living room of its furniture and installed countertops and shelves. The corner grocery store offered credit and home delivery. It stayed open late. At times it also served as a neighborhood political headquarters where governors, senators and congressmen dropped in to debate the latest issues.

Sanchez children and grandchildren live in the house now and run the little store. The latest generation has added its own philosophical touch to the storefront. On the Mesquite Street side of the building, a hand-lettered quote by John Ruskin sums up their sunny outlook— "The highest reward for a man's toil is not what he gets for it, but what he becomes by it."

Gonzales House

443 East May Avenue, Las Cruces
1910

The homes in the Mesquite District bear a distinct family resemblance—small, simple *adobes* crowded against sidewalks. But in the old section of Las Cruces, there is no mistaking one house for another. One is stuccoed pale blue, while a fanciful front porch shades another. Over one door a decorative tile pays homage to the Virgin of Guadalupe. A rock and wrought-iron entry sets one house apart from its plainer neighbor.

Nowhere is that individuality more evident than at the parapet, the low protective wall that extends above the flat roof. An architectural survey of the district reported no less than 13 different parapet styles. The parapet design of the Primitivo Gonzales house is particularly unique. The gentle curves of the undulating parapet are borrowed from the California Mission style. The brick coping is a Territorial feature usually reserved for level parapets. In another creative touch, the *canale* openings are tiled. *Canales*, or roof drains, are usually of tin or wood.

Dolan House

Main Street, Lincoln
Circa 1884

Lincoln looks like a stage set. Its one narrow street curves slightly past a two-story courthouse perfect for its part. Trees shade set-piece houses against the noonday sun. In Lincoln the drama once was very real, the set still is.

The Dolan house, for example, dates from Lincoln's heyday in the mid-1880s. Today, it is as appreciated for its classic Territorial architecture as it is famous for its owner, James J. Dolan. By the time Dolan completed this house in about 1884, he had survived the Lincoln County War, lost his business, rebuilt his fortune, and had been elected Lincoln County treasurer.

Dolan, an Irish immigrant, had come to New Mexico with the U.S. Army after the Civil War. In 1869 he was discharged at Fort Stanton, a few miles west of Lincoln on the Rio Bonito. Fort Stanton initially provided the settlers protection from Indian raids as well as a ready market for their grain, beef and lumber. Soon the military market expanded to include the Mescalero Apaches, who under treaty, received government rations at Fort Stanton. When he left the army, Dolan clerked for Lawrence Murphy, a former major stationed at Fort Stanton and one of several enterprising veterans engaged in ruthless competition for government contracts.

Economic rivalry and general lawlessness culminated in the Lincoln County War of 1878. On one side was the Murphy-Dolan faction, backed by Sheriff George Peppin and fifteen hired guns. The other side was led by a lawyer named Alexander McSween whose faction consisted of assorted farmers, ranchers and cowboys, plus a few gunfighters of their own—one nicknamed Billy the Kid. For five days in July 1878, the two sides waged war using Lincoln's one main street as their battleground. When it was over, McSween lay dead, his house torched. The Kid escaped through the flames. The story of the Lincoln County War eventually became the Saga of Billy the Kid, recounted in thick fictions, "B" movies, and even a ballet.

Sheriff Peppin went on to build fine houses in Lincoln, including the one for James Dolan. Peppin, who had been stationed at Fort Stanton as a private under Maj. Murphy, undoubtedly was inspired by the fort's Greek Revival style. The Dolan house features the best in Territorial touches, including the square columns of the front porch and the symmetrical placement of the windows. Peppin, a stone mason from Vermont, put his signature on all his houses, using shale plaster to give texture to the *adobe* walls.

Following the Lincoln County War, James J. Dolan turned his attention to rebuilding his business and his reputation. He became a successful merchant and rancher, and in 1888 was elected to the Territorial Senate. From all accounts, he lived the rest of his life as an honorable citizen.

Shuler House

436 Rio Grande Avenue, Ratón

1882

During the last days of February 1878, two railroads raced toward Ratón Pass, the 7,800-foot breach in the Ratón Mountains on the New Mexico-Colorado border. In a legal free-for-all, the first to begin construction at the pass would claim the right-of-way. The Atchison, Topeka and Santa Fe Railroad pushed west from Kansas, aiming for Santa Fe and the Pacific Coast beyond. Meanwhile, the Denver & Rio Grande was laying narrow-gauge track south from Colorado's mining towns, intent on capturing the coveted route. In a midnight coup, Ray Morley, a bold and charismatic engineer for the Santa Fe, armed his crew (plus a few recruits from a late-night dance) with picks and shovels and put them to work at the pass. By the time their rivals showed up at daylight, the Santa Fe Railroad had won the race.

In December, the first engine crested Ratón Pass chuffing steam into the thin air like modern-day smoke signals announcing a new era in New Mexico history. A few miles below at a watering hole and forage stop on the Santa Fe Trail, the town of Ratón was born. Its streets paralleled the railroad tracks, and its business was railroad business.

Because Ratón's early residents had no Southwestern heritage, they fashioned their homes after an assortment of architectural styles from the East and Midwest that became known as the Railroad style. The railroad not only imported the idea of what homes should look like, it also transported the materials to build them.

Dr. James Jackson Shuler arrived in Ratón in 1881 by way of Virginia, Kansas and New York. The next year he built this Queen Anne, a style full of unpredictable angles and Victorian variety. His two-story house of wood couldn't have been in greater contrast to the symmetry and the understated earthiness of the Territorial style. Just as the railroad had followed and then replaced the old Santa Fe Trail, so had the railroad ended the rein of the Territorial style.

Hobbs House

666 Cook Avenue, Ratón
1905

By the turn of the century, Ratón was a prospering town. Sheep and cattle by the thousands were shipped from its railyards to markets in Kansas City, St. Louis and Chicago. The newly developed coal fields in the nearby Ratón Mountains were a ready source of fuel for the Santa Fe's coal-fired steam engines. To Ratón's business district came railroaders, ranchers and miners where along First Street they bought supplies, stayed in hotels, and frequented restaurants and saloons with equal enthusiasm.

Ratón's prosperity also benefitted architects Isaac Hamilton Rapp and William Morris Rapp, brothers who had followed the railroad into New Mexico a decade earlier. They were originally from Carbondale, Illinois, where their father as well as five of his seven sons were architects. By 1905 when Alva Hobbs, a successful Ratón hardware dealer, commissioned them to build his house, the brothers headed the most prominent architectural firm in the Territory. Their practice was devoted mainly to public buildings, which they built in an array of styles that ranged from Georgian and Romanesque on the one end and Pueblo and Territorial on the other.

The Hobbs house, yellow trimmed in white, follows the Georgian style from its gabled dormer windows to its columned porch. The style was named for the three Kings George whose reigns coincided with the American colonial period. Stately and formal, the style lent itself to public buildings and mansions. Georgian, classed as a "masculine" style, tends to be blocky with strong architectural elements. For example, these dormer windows (capped with "broken" pediments) nearly shout "George Washington slept here."

Although interest in the style was patriotically rekindled during the nation's centennial, Georgian Revival eventually fell out of favor in New Mexico—but only after the Rapps had built New Mexico's capitol building and the governor's mansion in true Georgian fashion. These, too, would succumb to the vagaries of architectural trends. Both eventually were demolished and replaced by buildings designed in what later became known as the "Santa Fe Style," the regional style made popular by one Isaac Hamilton Rapp.

Ward House

403 Eighth Street, Las Vegas
1883

On the Fourth of July 1879 spectators gathered on the hillsides outside Las Vegas waiting to see the first train come to town. Children romped in the grass while parents kept vigil from buckboards and hay wagons. Nearby, cowboys soothed their skittish horses. The train's distant whistle at first quieted the crowd then sent them cheering as the locomotive, draped in evergreens and red, white and blue bunting, pulled into view.

Later "Old Town" residents would celebrate the historic event with a ball at the Exchange Hotel on the Las Vegas plaza. A mile east in new-town Las Vegas, others would attend a separate ball at one of the new frame buildings on Railroad Avenue. The dual celebrations marked not only the coming of the railroad, but also the beginning of political, cultural—as well as architectural—divisions between the old town and the new. While those in old town Las Vegas had built with *adobe*, newcomers were building with stone and brick and timber.

When James H. Ward, a contractor with the Santa Fe Railroad, came to Las Vegas in 1879, he settled easily in the new town. In 1883 he built a house in the fashionable neighborhood of Lincoln Park, in a fittingly fashionable style—Italianate. Patterned after the villas of the Italian countryside, Italianate in earlier decades had been the rage among America's monied class back East.

Ward must have followed a checklist of Italianate features when building his house. The focal point of the two-story brownstone is its square entrance tower, Italianate's defining characteristic. The tower, called a *campanile*, reaches beyond the roof line where a cast-iron railing crowns the Mansard roof. The balcony and fence railings, original and intact, repeat the theme.

The house is built of ashlar stonework, meaning the blocks are precision-cut and fitted. Dark sandstone (hence the term "brownstone") gives the house a textured, solid look. Lighter sandstone provides creamy accents in the window and door arches, at the corner blocks, called quoins, and along the foundation. The quality of the workmanship is due to an influx of stone workers and skilled stone cutters (the 1895 city directory lists 26) who quarried and cut local sandstone to build houses, churches, and other public buildings.

Ward himself went on to build two other stone houses in the neighborhood, but none achieved the devotion to style as did his own home, which today remains one of New Mexico's finest Italianate structures.

Gehring House

1103 Eighth Street, Las Vegas
1899

The Gehring house, built after the railroad had crisscrossed New Mexico in the 1880s, looks akin to both the Santa Fe depots and the Harvey Houses that dotted railroad towns across the West. The style is called California Mission, named for the *adobe* churches Spanish priests built throughout California. The railroad adapted the style, which included arches, tile roofs and curved parapets, in designing its depots. Fred Harvey, a freight agent turned restauranteur, in an agreement with the railroad built restaurants and hotels along the rail lines, giving them a California Mission look that closely identified them with the depots. In turn, local builders copied the style of Harvery's commercial buildings for their houses.

The Gehring house proudly displays the curved parapets of the California Mission style, along with its own whimsy—green glazed bricks scattered like confetti against a buff-colored background.

Harris House

1023 Seventh Street, Las Vegas
Circa 1900

The Harris house follows the tenets of scale and classic simplicity that have made American Colonial Revival the most popular style in American history. The original New England colonials were compact houses built of wood whose flat facades and gambrel roofs gave them the look of miniature barns. The style's revival was sparked by the 1876 Centennial and the nation's first attempt at historic preservation. Around the turn of the century, as homeowners began to tire of Victorian excess, the relatively unadorned American Colonial became more appealing.

Painted pale gold and trimmed in white, the Harris house is warm and inviting. The curved roof of the eye-catching entry rests on solid porch columns, while a fan-shaped Palladian window peeks out from above. The gambrel roof is cross-gabled, a feature found in only about ten percent of its New England predecessors.

While American Colonial seems out of place in New Mexico, its homey style is well-suited to families. A century after it was built, the Harris house is still full of the sounds of family life—supper dishes being cleared from the table, the practice notes of someone at the piano.

Ilfeld House

1053 Eighth Street, Las Vegas
1908-1913

Until the twentieth century, Americans had a fondness for naming house styles after English monarchs. The queens Victoria and Anne, three Georges and one James all contributed to the lexicon of American architecture. Though the architectural style named for King James I—Jacobean—is the least-known, the king himself left his share of historic footnotes. James I was not only the son of Mary Queen of Scots, and the man who authorized the King James Version of the Bible, he also was the reigning Stuart who authorized the colonization of North America. Jamestown, the first permanent English settlement in America, bears his name.

The Jacobean style is typified by steep roof gables, fine brickwork, and towering chimneys. Jacobean, which was associated with old-world class and wealth, was a fitting choice for Arthur Ilfeld's elegant brick mansion in Las Vegas. Arthur was heir to a family of wealth and accomplishment. His father, Charles Ilfeld, was a Jewish merchant who in 1865 opened a mercantile store on the Las Vegas Plaza. By 1890 Charles Ilfeld had become a leading merchant in the Territory. His mercantile business now included a three-story stone building on the plaza, three warehouses and eleven branch stores. By then Las Vegas, a beneficiary of the railroad boom, was enjoying a brief reign as New Mexico's largest city.

Hesselden House

1211 Roma NW, Albuquerque

1882

Albuquerque secured its place in New Mexico's history the day José Leandro Perea tried to outfox the railroad. The exchange between the representatives of the Santa Fe Railroad and Perea, a Bernalillo sheep rancher, was cool and brief. They offered Perea $2 to $3 an acre for the right of way through his vast land holdings. The same price held for land on the eastern outskirts of Bernalillo that the railroad wanted for offices and railyards. With hardly a blink, the proud Don José, a millionaire two times over, countered at $425 an acre. The delegation headed straight for Albuquerque.

Albuquerque was more than prepared to grant concessions to the Santa Fe. Here, the town fathers included not only the descendants of Spanish colonists, but also the sons of German, Irish, Polish and French immigrants who saw the railroad as crucial to New Mexico's economic and social progress. Three of these men—Franz Huning, William Hazeldine and Elias Stover—served as agents for the New Mexico Town Company, a subsidiary of the Santa Fe Railroad. The agents bought huge sections of bargain-priced land along the path of the railroad. Once the railroad was established, the company sold off its surplus land, now commercially valuable, at a fine profit of which the agents received half.

Such lands were the farm fields that lay between the original Albuquerque townsite and the Santa Fe tracks a mile and a half east. Once the railroad arrived in 1880, the fields quickly filled with a grid of parallel streets, and the streets with the businesses and homes of the new Albuquerque.

One of its first homes was the Hesselden house, a two-story of red sandstone built in 1882. Its low-hipped bracketed roof identifies the house as Italianate. The rough, irregular cut stonework contrasts with the smooth precision of ashlar stonework of the Ward house in Las Vegas. The south side of the house faces street side, with the bay windows likely added later to catch the winter sun. Today, the west front faces a neighboring house, but a century ago the house had an unbroken view across the farm fields of José Leandro Perea.

Edward Lembke House

416 Walter SE, Albuquerque
1896

In 1880 when Franz Huning platted Albuquerque's first subdivision just east of the railroad tracks, he named the first few streets after members of his family—Edith, Arno, and Walter. Over the next decades the homes in the Huning Highlands Addition came to reflect Huning's vision for the new Albuquerque.

One of its early residents was Edward Lembke, a brickmason who in 1896 built his house on Walter Street from pug-mill bricks manufactured in his back yard. In this age-old brickmaking process, brick clay was churned (mule-power turned the paddles) in a huge wooden box called a "pug mill." Dollops of brick "dough" were then patted into molds and turned out to dry. The sun-dried bricks were then stacked over a wood fire for hardening.

By the turn of the century the neighborhood had begun to fill with homey Victorian-style houses, many built with Lembke's bricks. (The bricks in the Lembke house since have been stuccoed over.) For his own home, which he lived in until 1956, Lembke chose the style called Free Classic Queen Anne, so named for its classical porch columns. The style is a hybrid of sorts, replacing the delicate spindle work of Queen Anne with the sturdy columns borrowed from the Colonial Revival style.

By mid-century the homes in Huning Highlands represented a variety of revived styles—Colonial, Pueblo and Mediterranean—as well as apartments, bungalows, and even some tuberculosis cottages whose screened porches let in the pure, high-altitude air believed to have curative powers. But the lure of newer neighborhoods, the Depression and two World Wars had left Huning Highlands ragged at the edges. The larger homes had been subdivided into apartments, while smaller ones had fallen into neglect. In addition, hundreds of houses had been demolished to make way for Interstate 25.

The 1970s, however, saw a resurging appreciation for the old neighborhood. New owners took on the hard task of restoration. They also renewed the spirit of neighborliness with block parties, historic home tours, Victorian Fairs and a Dickens Christmas progressive dinner. In 1978 Huning Highlands became Albuquerque's first historic district to be listed on the National Register of Historic Places.

Ann Carson and her husband, Jim, bought the Lembke house when they moved to Albuquerque from California in 1978. Like many of their neighbors, their participation in historic preservation begins at home and extends to the entire neighborhood. In this photograph, Ann's painting of Huning Highlands homes is on temporary exhibition in front of the house. The art work, painted with house paint, is displayed during the holiday season each year. Her other handiwork is the white picket fence, which was reproduced based on early photographs of the home, and which she and Jim painted picket-by-picket.

Cornish House

123 Walter SE, Albuquerque
Circa 1901

Dr. P.G. Cornish, Sr., was known in Albuquerque as one of the "Four Horsemen"—four horse-and-buggy physicians always hurrying through the city's streets or into the countryside to treat patients. With such a demanding practice, it is likely that Dr. Cornish built his home on Walter Street with convenience in mind. His house, located in the heart of Albuquerque's first subdivision, was a few blocks east of the train station, and a couple of miles from Albuquerque's Old Town.

The Cornish house is a simplified version of a Second Empire Mansard—Second Empire for Napoleon III, and Mansard after Francois Mansart, the greatest French architect of his day (his day being the 1600s). Paris exhibitions in the mid-1800s showcased the Mansard roof, which the English popularized and the Americans adopted. The typical Mansard roof consists of a steep lower slope and a gently angled, almost flat top portion. The lower roof often followed straight lines, but depending on the local fashion, it could flare, curve in, curve out, or curve in *and* out.

The Cornish house is an unusual Mansard style in that its upper roof is hipped, ending with an iron railing bordering the flat roof top. The lower roof, however, retains its Mansard quirkiness, sloping away in four planes, three with dipped gabled dormers. Exceptionally wide curving eaves give the house a look of its own—that of a giant cookie jar, hand-painted in Victorian blue and dark green.

McCoy House

901 North Rio Grande, Aztec

1895

Like many of Aztec's early settlers, Will and Ella Ann McCoy lived in a cabin built from cottonwood logs and roofed in sod. It was a suitable house, made homey by Ella Ann's fine quilts. But when a roof leak soaked the quilts in muddy water, she decided the matter without debate. Ella Ann told her husband firmly, "Build me a house that does not leak." And so he did.

In 1895 in the orchard he had planted with apple trees, and near the irrigation ditch he had helped build, Will built a sturdy brick cottage with a hipped roof steep enough to shed rain and snow. Its walls were of double brick and its foundation of sandstone. The symmetry of the house and the (slightly off center) Queen Anne porch identify it as Folk Victorian. The style was popular from about 1870 to 1910 during the time the railroad was crossing the continent, leaving in its wake both new ideas of home styles and the material to build them.

With their house finished, the McCoys continued the energetic lives common to pioneers. Will's orchard produced peaches, cherries and apples. In 1903, two years before the narrow gage railroad reached Aztec, Will hauled 3,000 boxes of apples to Durango, Colorado, building fires around the wagons at night to keep the apples from freezing. Later, he shipped fruit to Durango on the train dubbed the Red Apple Flyer. Will also owned a hardware store and ran cattle. Often while he was at a round-up Ella Ann and their daughters took care of irrigating the orchard.

Today, the house is well-loved and well-cared for by a McCoy greatgrandson, although only a single apple tree remains of the orchard. Meanwhile, the irrigation ditch, now more than a century old, nourishes yet another season of ditch-bank flowers.

Luna Mansion

When Santa Fe Railroad officials requested a right-of-way through Antonio José Luna's property, he generously deeded it over. The right-of-way, after all, would take but a sliver from the hundreds of thousands of acres the Luna family owned. Unfortunately, the proposed railroad tracks would run straight through the Luna *hacienda*. In compensation, the railroad agreed to build the Lunas a new house in keeping with their status as one of New Mexico's most wealthy and politically prominent families.

It is said the Lunas modeled their new home after the southern mansions they had visited during their travels in the South. The feel, if not the look, of the plantation South is evident in the grand house they designed. The original house was built in 1881, in the Italianate style, which about that time was nearing the end of its run as the national favorite. The hooded floor-length windows, the arching bay windows, and the thick bracketed eaves all are Italianate trimmings. The hipped roof, also indicative of Italianate, is sheathed in tin and painted to look like copper. The mansion's smooth exterior hides 18 inches of straw-stabilized *adobe*.

Because Don Antonio José died the year the mansion was completed, his son Tranquilino was the first to occupy the house. In the early 1900s title to the house passed to Tranquilino's nephew Eduardo Otero. Eduardo's wife, Josefita Manderfield Otero, as the new mistress of the mansion, poured her creative energies into the house and its gardens. Josefita herself was a woman of substance whose father, William R. Manderfield, had founded the *Santa Fe New Mexican*.

With a flair for the dramatic, she replaced the one-story wooden porch with a columned portico that reached the full height of the house. Turning again to the South for inspiration, she built the portico in the Greek Revival style, which down South went by the name of Southern Colonial. The Tuscan columns, smooth and classically Roman, are antebellum hallmarks. A pilaster, a shallow type of column, lies flat against the back wall giving the porch depth.

The porch is a welcoming entry for patrons of the restaurant that now occupies the Luna mansion. They dine in luxury and quiet conversation, surrounded by Josefita's paintings of cherubs and maidens. But once in a while, the reverie is broken by the rumble of a freight train, passing on schedule just a block away.

Jackson House

1700 Ninth Street, Alamogordo
Circa 1902

A P. Jackson's gray two-story house—all wood, windows and paint—is appropriate for the founder of a chain of lumber yards. Two years after he built the house, he and partner Harry Galbraith formed the Alamogordo-based Jackson-Galbraith Co. The house, true to the style called Free Classic Queen Anne, features fluted columns, palladian windows and colored glass transoms.

Jackson built the house in 1902 just four years after railroad promoter Charles B. Eddy created the townsite he christened *Alamogordo*, roughly "big cottonwood" in Spanish. No matter that the town had no trees, Eddy shipped in 44,000 pounds of cottonwood trees and planted them along the street facing the railroad tracks. Back then, the railroad meant big business to lumbering. Eddy's railroad spur to Cloudcroft east of Alamogordo tapped into the rich timber lands of the Sacramento Mountains. The mountain pines provided construction lumber for Jackson's company as well as railroad ties and bridge timbers for Eddy's El Paso and Northeastern Railway.

Thompson House

409 West Las Cruces Avenue, Las Cruces
1909

The street that fronts the Thompson house dead ends a few blocks west where it bumps into the boarded-up Santa Fe Railroad depot. Las Cruces Avenue, once called Depot Avenue, was the first paved street in town, a civic improvement designed to impress arriving passengers. Almost from the day the railroad reached Las Cruces in 1881, the Depot District attracted the town's newly arrived and newly powerful who built homes there in a perfect variety of styles.

On the day they married, Mark and Edith Georgia Thompson received a house lot on Depot Avenue as a wedding gift from her parents. The location was ideal. It was near the depot and just a block from the Doña Ana County Courthouse, where Thompson served as district attorney.

In 1909 the newlyweds built a one-story stuccoed adobe in the Western Stick style, a California variation of the widely popular Craftsman style. Craftsman is defined by structural simplicity—open eaves, wide roof overhang, and exposed rafter ends. About 1903 in Pasadena, two brothers, Charles and Henry Greene, replaced the heaviness of Craftsman with a blend of Spanish and Oriental elements to produce high-style wooden architecture. At first, Spanish and Oriental styles seem a strange pairing. On second thought, the rafter ends of the Thompson house *do* resemble Spanish carved corbels *and* with a slight upward curve, they would be perfectly at home on a Japanese bungalow.

The Thompsons sold their two-bedroom house in 1917, which by then was too small for their family of four children. Through the years, however, a succession of owners has carefully preserved the integrity of the house. Also, the old Santa Fe depot is in the early stages of restoration. When the depot is completed, the neighborhood around it will fulfill the promise town fathers hoped for in 1881.

Boxcar House

Derry Street, Rincón

When the Santa Fe Railroad selected Rincón as a junction in 1881, it never intended the former stage stop to become a railroad town. Simply, Rincón provided a convenient site for the railroad's engine house, depot, and later a Harvey House dining room.

Within a month, however, 40 businesses, including hotels, restaurants and several saloons, had set up shop near and sometimes on railroad property. Homes, mostly adobes and *jacales*, also crowded the railyards, leading railroad officials in 1882 to order the residents off the property. The order caused *The Prospector*, a mining journal in nearby Hillsboro to huff: "The railroad wants the residents of Rincón to build their new houses on wheels so that they can move when the company decides how much land it wants." Despite the railroad's lack of enthusiasm, Rincón continued to grow, adding a barbershop, two general stores, and a drugstore to its list of businesses. A housing shortage prompted the railroad to outfit several boxcars to rent to its own employees.

But in the spring and summer of 1884, a flooding Rio Grande halted Rincón's boisterous growth. In a disastrous lack of foresight, the railroad had built its facilities on the river valley floor at a point where the river took a sharp turn. (*Rincón* means corner in Spanish.) In June the railroad lost three engines and several boxcars to the raging waters. Just south of Rincón, the flooding river washed an engine and two flatcars, carrying 20 track repairmen, into the drink. The men swam to safety but the engine and flatcars were beyond rescue.

That fall the railroad moved to higher ground a mile north, this time reluctantly agreeing to include a townsite in its plans. At the news, a Las Cruces newspaper reported that now ". . .Rincón can afford to build fine houses and put on airs, like other American towns." But it never did.

Today, Rincón is nearly a ghost town. The Harvey House is gone. So are the hotels. The railroad depot and a one-room post office stand as Rincón's only proof of viability. Mobile homes are scattered among simple adobe and frame houses. On Derry Street a boxcar house, recently vacated in favor of an *adobe* home, is a weathered memento of the time Rincón wanted to be a railroad town.

Ailman House

312 West Broadway, Silver City
1881

In the early 1870s Henry B. Ailman built his first house in Silver City from leftover adobes abandoned by another miner in a hurry. The 10 by 12 foot cabin would have to suffice until Ailman struck silver he hoped to find "sticking out of the ground" in the hills of nearby Georgetown.

Ailman certainly wasn't the first optimist with a fever for silver and gold. Had not Coronado, based on dubious but enthusiastic reports, traipsed across the Southwest looking for the Seven Cities of Gold? And despite Coronado's failure, had not Don Juan de Oñate set out to colonize New Mexico in 1598 fully equipped with tools for mining and smelting ore? Just in case.

As it turned out, Ailman hit pay dirt. He and his partner, Hartford Meredith, developed the richest silver mine in Georgetown. The partners then sold the mine for $160,000 and used the money to build lucrative merchandising and banking businesses in Silver City. In 1881 across the street from Ailman's little adobe, the men built fine brick houses that were exact duplicates of each other.

Ailman's house (shown here) was a Queen Anne of fanciful architectural variety. The Italianate brick tower came with four lookout windows. The bellshaped Mansard roof, for emphasis, was banded in forest green fishscale shingles. A dormer above and bay window below added to the mix. Finally, chamfered posts—their corners beveled at 45 degree angles—propped up the porch, aided by the turned spindle railing.

The house today is trimmed in muted gold, a color based on a sampling of historic paints from the building. Color was an essential element in Queen Anne houses. The spectrum ranged from dignified shades of warm, neutral colors, such as the gold used on the Ailman house, to the deep greens, robin's egg blues, Indian reds, and the occasional purple used on houses dubbed "painted ladies" for their lively colors.

The local newspaper pronounced the twin houses as "decidedly the most stylish private residences in town." However, Silver City's fortunes began to slide in 1883, crashing for Ailman and Meredith in December 1887. Bank losses cost them their businesses and their twin homes. Both men eventually left Silver City. In 1905 Meredith's house was moved a few blocks away, its exterior remodeled to simplicity. Ailman's house, still thoroughly Victorian, since 1967 has housed the Silver City Museum.

Warren House

105 East Market Street, Silver City
1885

In 1882 Orange Scott and Elizabeth Warren arrived in Silver City ready to settle down with their three young children. O.S. quickly tapped into the mining and ranching boom to build a successful insurance and real estate business. Then in 1885, at age thirty-eight, he died of a heart attack. Elizabeth was thirty-one.

With hardly a misstep, Mrs. Warren took up her husband's business, incorporating a large corner office for herself in their new home. The house was built of local red brick in the Italianate style. Italianate proved a natural choice for the Warren home, as it reflected both personal prosperity and Silver City's identity as a "real American town." Inside, Mrs. Warren's home was Victorian by design, all wainscot and wallpaper. Instead of the dark, heavily draped look favored in that era, large floor-to-ceiling windows gave the house an open, airy disposition.

Over the next 25 years the innovative and energetic Mrs. Warren wrote more insurance policies than any other agent in the Southwest. Along the way she bought real estate all over Silver City, including rental property and undeveloped town lots.

She also fought floods that came almost yearly. When the flood of 1902 hit, she organized a sandbagging crew to shore up the crumbling bank in front of her house. Then in 1907 she went into a business that would provide more protection than sandbags—concrete. First she consulted her friend Matlida Koehler, whose brother had been a concrete contractor. Then she persuaded her friend to quit her position as school principal to supervise sidewalk building. Before long, Silver City was treated to the sight of Mrs. Warren, little more than five feet tall, and Miss Koehler, at six feet, outfitted in work shoes and culottes.

Using the know-how from sidewalk construction, they next challenged the Big Ditch, Main Street's more descriptive name. They used stone cut from Mrs. Warren's own quarry, lumber from her own sawmill, plus the labor of 300 men to build a 200-foot-long retaining wall along the ditch bank in front of the Warren house. Successive floods have since scoured Main Street to its bedrock, 50 feet below, washing away every single Main Street building save one—the Warren house.

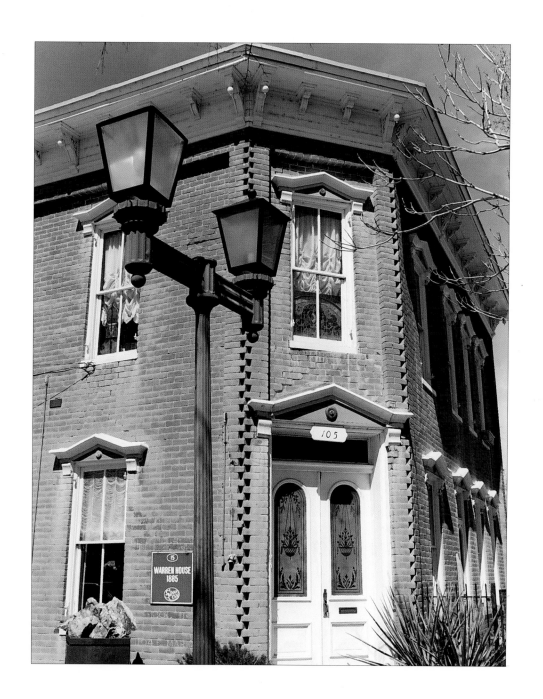

Marriott House

615 West Sixth Street, Silver City
1906

Oh, to be invited to the Marriotts' for the Fourth of July! Mr. and Mrs. C.W. Marriott loved to entertain and had built their new house with hospitality in mind. Mr. Marriott, a former Wells Fargo Express agent, appeared to have done quite well with his own freight line to the Mogollon mines. For the party, the Marriotts would have hung red, white and blue bunting from the porch railing in patriotic welcome to their guests. A young woman, hair piled in Gibson Girl fashion, likely would have been serving lemonade from an artfully balanced tray. From the turreted corner of the veranda (its conical roof is now gone), Mr. Marriott would have been holding forth on the idea of using trucks instead of mule teams to haul freight.

The Marriotts, like many middle-class families in small-town America, preferred the homey informality of the Queen Anne style.

Queen Anne was named and popularized by a group of English architects whose work was transported to the United States in the 1870s. Theirs was an odd choice of monarchs considering that Queen Anne, described as a conscientious and simple soul, reigned from 1702 to 1714 when cathedral building was more the vogue. Regardless, Americans warmed to Queen Anne, adding spindlework or paring it to simpler lines as it suited them.

The Marriotts chose the simplified version, sometimes referred to as Free Classic Queen Anne. Simplified but not simple. Dormer windows, for example, peak from the roof as they please, their gable ends studded with carved sunbursts. But it is the wraparound veranda, with its whimsical turret, that surely charmed the Marriotts most.

Esquibel House

406 South Pinos Altos Street, Silver City
Circa 1905

In the 1870s a group of Mexican miners arrived in Silver City hoping to trade their skills for the rewards of work, if not riches, from the silver mines in the surrounding hills. They left behind a Mexico dizzied by revolution and reform and an economy enfeebled by played-out mines. For their new homes these immigrants from the Mexican state of Chihuahua found familiar terrain—a rough, barren hill at the south end of town. Anglos also emulated their former home towns by laying out Silver City's Main Street on a north-south axis. They later regretted the decision when floods turned Main Street into an arroyo 50 feet deep.

By 1873 Hispanics in Silver City numbered about 700, double that of the Anglo population. Many of the Hispanic families, though not all, had settled on Chihuahua Hill where the rocky soil supplied a handy source of building materials. There, *adobe* houses, stores and *cantinas* were scattered helter-skelter over the hillsides. These residents had in effect recreated their old neighborhoods in their new homeland. The early residents of Socorro, Las Cruces and Roswell also settled in *Chihuahuita*, or little Chihuahua, neighborhoods.

In 1905, about the time the Esquibel house was built, Chihuahua Hill residents had begun to trade their leak-prone flat roofs for gabled ones made of tin. Some also added fanciful Victorian touches to their simple houses. The Esquibel house, for example, wears its Queen Anne style porch as easily as lace on a bonnet. The balustrade's spindlework posts and the fretwork brackets no doubt were mail-order imports. (Note that the posts at the center and end of the porch have been replaced by plain wooden slats.) By the time this version of Queen Anne worked its way west, the style had gone from being called Folk Victorian, to Western Victorian, to New Mexico Vernacular.

Medical Staff Quarters

Fort Bayard
1910

Fort Bayard is as still as dawn. Tree branches throw long shadows across old colonial houses as if in shielding their occupants from the rising sun, they prolong the hour before reveille. But reveille will not sound today. Instead, the day begins with the time clock, a click in the quiet routine of caretakers.

Fort Bayard was established in 1866, the year Congress authorized the army to establish six all-Black regiments, composed mostly of soldiers who had served in the Civil War. Congress reasoned that Black soldiers could be used on the frontier to subdue the Indians, plus the Blacks would be far removed from the nervous prejudices of postwar America. Fort Bayard seemed far enough.

In the next two decades, the Black troops at Fort Bayard divided their time between fort building and Indian chasing. During that time, the soldiers built living quarters for 400 men, plus a commissary, corrals, a hospital a-story-and-a-half high, a guardhouse, a bakery and a magazine. In a clearing of pines they marked off precise rows for a cemetery.

Their main duty, however, was to protect settlers and miners from the Indians. The mines at nearby Pinos Altos and Santa Rita lay on lands of the wide-ranging Apaches. Despite fierce resistance against the army, the loss of their leaders (Mangas Colorado, killed in 1863; Victorio, dead in 1880; Geronimo, captured in 1886), eventually cost them their lands.

With the Indian threat gone, the army began withdrawing troops from Fort Bayard, turning the fort over to the U.S. Army Surgeon General. In 1899 Fort Bayard and Fort Stanton (near Lincoln) became the first federal tuberculosis treatment centers in the United States. At that time, doctors believed that fresh air, particularly at high altitudes, would cure tuberculosis. Fort Bayard's 400-bed hospital, sitting at 6,180 feet, was well-equipped for "altitude therapy."

During the next decade, the army replaced worn-out , outdated adobe, frame and pine log buildings with larger, sturdier models. In 1910 the old military garrison buildings were replaced with a row of two-story Colonial Revival style duplexes to house the medical staff. At times, as many as 1,700 tuberculosis patients—active duty soldiers and sailors—were treated at Fort Bayard's hospital.

Today, the quiet at Fort Bayard is serene, somehow comforting. The hospital now belongs to the state of New Mexico, which uses it to care for aged patients. Just over the hill in a clearing of pines is the National Cemetery where granite headstones are set in rows laid out so long ago.

Miller House

Elenora Street, Hillsboro
1894

This is the house that sits in the town that gold built. This is a house, in fact, built from the remains of smelted gold. In 1894 on a hill overlooking town, Hillsboro's smelter was running full-force separating gold from its molten brew. Slag, the leavings of this process, was poured into forms where it cooled to a black iridescence. Like remnants of a rainbow, the purplish pinks, blues and greens must have caught the fancy of George and Ninette Miller. For on the opposite hill, the Millers built their house of slag blocks and trimmed it in Queen Anne details.

Hillsboro traces its beginnings to April 1877 when a couple of prospectors discovered gold in the Mimbres Range. Their discovery set off a mini-gold rush and Hillsboro was born four months later. By the end of the year the gulches around Hillsboro were swarming with prospectors looking for placer gold. In its heyday, the Hillsboro mining district produced $6 million in silver and gold.

By the time the Millers built their house, Hillsboro had progressed from boom town to county seat. It was a family town by then, with children accounting for a quarter of its 400 residents. As with many mining towns, Hillsboro was an immigrant community. Mexico accounted for about half of the immigrants, with Ireland and England leading the numbers coming from Europe. By the turn of the century, Hillsboro's fortunes declined along with those of other mining towns in New Mexico. Perhaps because Hillsboro had built a community with schools and churches, it never succumbed to ghost town status. Today, Hillsboro is a shady retreat for retirees and writers, a place where the post office still draws a crowd at delivery time. The Miller house sits perched on the hill, its fishscale shingles painted in bright pink, rust and turquoise. It is still the only house in town that started out as gold dust.

Garcia/Bursum House

326 Church Street, Socorro

1887

Holm O. Bursum was a man of vigor and ambition who chose a Victorian house that equalled him in its drama and take-notice style. Both he and Victorian architecture arrived in New Mexico about the same time. In 1880, Bursum—as a thirteen-year-old orphan—had wandered into Ratón, a brand-new railroad town alive with activity. The young Bursum no doubt took note of Ratón's freshly minted Victorians. Years later, he would buy one for his own.

In 1880 the railroad also arrived in Socorro, ushering in the town's most prosperous era. Above all, the railroad proved a boon for the fledgling mining industry. Although silver had been discovered in the Magdalena Mountains and at Socorro Peak in the late 1860s, ore had to be shipped over the Santa Fe Trail for smelting, an expense hardly worth the effort. But with the railroad's arrival, Socorro soon became the smelting center for New Mexico, as well as parts of Arizona, Texas, Utah and Mexico. At Socorro the raw ore was smelted into 100-pound bars of bullion, then shipped to St. Louis for further refining.

Candelario Garcia, a landowner and eleven-term veteran of the Territorial Legislature, was an obvious beneficiary of Socorro's new-found prosperity—obvious because of the fine Victorian he built in 1887. In 1899 Garcia sold the house to Holm Bursum.

Although the Bursum house followed basic Queen Anne styling, its Eastlake porch and brick construction made it a standout for its time. The style is named for Charles Eastlake, an English furniture designer whose generous use of spindlework was enthusiastically adopted in America. Eastlake touches also decorated the house's center cross gable as well as the twin gables of the porch.

By the time Bursum bought the house in Socorro, the thirty-two-year-old entrepreneur had made his way to San Antonio, some ten miles south of Socorro, where he worked for A.H. Hilton. He also had started his own business, secured a freighting contract at Fort Wingate, bought two ranches, served as the Socorro County sheriff, and was beginning his first term in the Territorial Legislature.

Bursum continued his frenetic political career, serving four terms as the mayor of Socorro while also leading the quest for New Mexico statehood. Although he failed to achieve higher office (he ran twice for governor and was thwarted by Albert Fall in a bid for the U.S. Senate), Bursum remained devoted to politics. During his long career in public life Bursum and his family maintained their home in Socorro. Mrs. Bursum sold the house after his death in 1952.

Miner's Cottage

11 Cave Road, Madrid
Circa 1900

Madrid is a renaissance town, brought from the brink of extinction by a group the press once described as "hippies and East Coast dropouts." Regardless, this new breed of settlers has transformed the old coal town into a shady stop for tourists meandering New Mexico's back roads.

Coal was first mined in the area in 1835, with Madrid's settlement dating to 1869. Later Madrid was a major supplier to the railroad. In 1919 Madrid was taken over by the Albuquerque and Cerrillos Coal Co., and for the next 35 years Madrid earned its livelihood as a company town. In addition to the mines, the company owned Madrid's general store, hospital, hotel, utilities, and amusement hall.

The company also owned all the houses—wooden miner's shacks that had been sawed into sections and hauled in on freight cars soon after the turn of the century. The company rented the stitched-together cottages to its workers for about $15 a month.

Life in this company town was not altogether grim. To keep its employees happy, occupied and out of the union during the hard times of the Depression, the company sponsored elaborate social and sports activities (funded by the company and Employee Club dues). Its Christmas celebration earned Madrid the title as the "Christmas City" of the Southwest. During the holidays a company-mandated Christmas tree was posted in every front yard, and 50,000 lights were strung from one end of town to the other. Trans World Airlines even rerouted flights so passengers could see the glittering "Christmas City" from the air.

Although the coal company survived the Great Depression, it failed to meet increasing competition from the oil and natural gas industries. Finally in 1954 The Albuquerque and Cerrillos Coal Co. closed down. The company put the entire town up for sale, including its 200 houses. For 20 years, while the company searched for a buyer to meet its asking price of $250,000, the town dwindled to a handful of residents and 150 buildings. In February 1975 individual buildings were put on the market. The board and batten miners' cottages sold out first, bringing between $1,500 and $7,500 each. Within 16 days, all 150 buildings had new owners. By May, Madrid boasted a population of 80.

An Italian who baked for the miners once lived in the cottage shown here. His granddaughter owns it now. Today, many of the other cottages are the homes of shopkeepers and artists. Often as not, the cottages are shops themselves. One, painted funky orange and black, sells something called Woo Wear. Another doubles as a pastry cafe and pottery shop where a couple in hiking boots sit drinking espresso. Out front, a tourist snaps a picture of a man in a scruffy gray beard, who looks for all the world like an old miner. As it turns out, he runs the grocery store.

Keil House

Keil Avenue and Railroad Avenue, Lake Valley
1883

The powdery bones of Judge William P. Keil lie in a grave in the Lake Valley cemetery, the exact location forgotten. Keil's old house, empty since his death in 1930, perhaps is a more fitting monument.

Judge Keil arrived in Lake Valley in the spring of 1882 hard on the heels of the richest silver strike in history. The discovery of the famed Bridal Chamber Mine the year before had transformed Lake Valley into a thriving mining town with a population that eventually would reach 4,000. In the midst of this activity, Keil occupied himself with a variety of professions, none of which was mining and none of which made him very much money. The house he built in 1883, a modest two-room *adobe* with wood floors and a tin roof, proved sufficient for his solitary needs. During the half century he served as Lake Valley's coroner and justice of the peace, the New Mexico Vernacular style house remained unchanged.

When the nation adopted the gold standard in 1893 the silver market dropped, taking Lake Valley and its silver-dependent economy down with it. Two years later most of Main Street burned to the ground. Even the lake dried up. After the bust, Keil became Lake Valley's caretaker of sorts, parceling out goods left behind and selling off houses abandoned in the exodus. When the old judge died, he was buried without ceremony in a second-hand grave.

Lake Valley today contains not a living soul.

Chavez/Lee House

5000 San Mateo Road, San Mateo
1876

The wide valley of the San Mateo Mountains is watered from underground where a volcanic shelf traps runoff for safekeeping. The Navajos knew this place as "The Meadows" for its thick grasses and stand of sheltering oaks. In about 1836 the oaks served as a landmark and a sanctuary for young Manuel Chavez, the lone survivor of a Navajo attack. Manuelito, slight and just sixteen, collapsed under the oaks where sleep soothed the delirium of his seven wounds. When he awoke, he knew he would live. One day he also would build a ranch in this valley, and under the very oaks where his life had been renewed, he would build his house.

By the time Manuel Chavez built his *hacienda*, he was nearing sixty and bone weary from a life led to the hilt. He was born under the Spanish flag, had served under Governor Armijo in Mexico's surrender to the Americans, then as a Union colonel, had helped destroy the Confederate supply train at Glorieta. Meanwhile he ranched sheep along the Pecos River and fought Indians on nearly every front.

Then in 1876 he joined his younger brother Román Baca at San Mateo where they built a sheep ranching empire of some 200,000 acres. It seemed a good life. Charles Lummis visited Chavez in 1885, reporting to his Ohio newspaper that the *hacienda* "is tastefully furnished in American style, handsomely papered and carpeted. The windows are hung with lace curtains, while the rugs and table-covers are precious Navajo blankets."

The Chavez family sold the ranch to Floyd Lee around 1919. Lee's wife, Francis, brightened the *hacienda* with color, filling windowpanes with her own hand-painted flowers. Their son, Harry, managed the ranch until his death in 1977. Today, Harry's widow, Iona Lee, lovingly preserves the history of the *hacienda*, which is now her home. She tends to the grapes that grow in the old *placita* (seen through the double doors from Floyd Lee's study) just as carefully as she presides over the ranch operations, now a cattle ranch of some 300,000 acres, run by her sons.

Mills House

509 First Street, Springer
1880

Melvin W. Mills was a cunning frontier lawyer who made a fortune representing clients ranging from outlaws, to land-grabbers, to the Territorial government. He also earned his share of enemies and wielded a good measure of influence. Twice he escaped lynch mobs, once with the U.S. Cavalry at his rescue. He used his political power to have the Colfax County seat moved to Springer just in time for the railroad's arrival. There he built a mansion in his own charmed, but rule-bending way.

In its pick-and-choose style, the mansion adopted the best of Mansard, Queen Anne and Territorial features. The Mansard roof is sheathed in sheet metal stamped to look like slate. Balustrades on the two wrap-around verandas showcase intricate versions of Queen Anne spindlework, once painted deep red and green. In a bow to regional influence, the pedimented window and door lintels are Territorial style.

The entry hall (right) though small for such a large house, was no less dramatic. Daylight through the ruby glass transom filled the hall with an ember-hot glow. At night, the ruby glass glowed from inside out. The staircase spiraled unbroken to the third floor, which also could be reached from a basement elevator. The Mills saga includes the spurious theory that Mills was a white slaver who used the elevator to transport young women to his third floor "prison" from the basement where a tunnel is rumored to lead to a house across the street. White slavery was known as a means of keeping frontier dance halls filled with young women.

Considering the company he kept, Mills lived a surprisingly long life. Even so, in 1925 he died broke, having lost his businesses, his ranches, and his mansion. Legend has it that his dying wish was to be carried into the mansion to die in his old room. Some say his wish was granted. Others say it was too late.

Reynolds Cabin

Main Street, Luna

1893

In 1882 two brothers driving a herd of cattle into northwestern New Mexico passed through a mountain valley so beautiful that when they returned home to Utah, they set to making plans for a Mormon settlement. Before winter was out, six families—including 22 children—arrived in the Luna Valley. The only hitch was that it was occupied by two trappers who obligingly agreed to sell their "claim" on the valley and two log cabins for $400.

A more serious complication was the arrival of the Luna brothers on March 26. The long-time sheep ranchers had come to inspect the land they had been using for summer pasture. They found instead a group of Mormons clearing the fields for planting. Although neither group had clear title to the land, under the Homestead Act, the Mormons held the upper hand. The Lunas, recognizing a losing proposition, withdrew their claim.

The Mormons then turned back to the tasks at hand. With most of their time devoted to clearing and planting, many lived in their covered wagons or in tents. Within the year, however, the settlement counted 26 log houses, 1 frame house, and 45 families. The Mormons voted to name their community Grant in honor of a church official. For good measure they also voted to change the name of Luna Valley to Pleasant Valley. However, the post office and tradition prevailing, both the town and the valley would be called Luna.

In July 1893 the settlers decided it was time for a church building. The little log church was completed four months later with Braman Reynolds named as sexton. Later the building (shown here) was converted into a house. In the 1930s a generation of Reynolds children were born and raised in the house. Although it doesn't look like much now, the wobbly old cabin still stands just east of the new Luna Ward Chapel.

Today, some 160 people live in Luna year around. It's a cheerful town of like-minded people given to telling stories on themselves. Their peculiar sense of humor, they say, makes them "Lunatics."

Kretek House

500 South Tin, Deming
1888

House styles hold clues to a city's history. A *viga* in Taos tells of its Pueblo past, while a pedimented window in Santa Fe shows its American heritage. A spindlework porch in any town harkens to the railroad era.

The Kretek house does not so easily yield its clues, but they are there nevertheless. For example, the ranch family that built the house in 1888 no doubt had need for its six bedrooms. Ranch families often moved into town so their children could attend school. As it happened, the year before, Deming had opened a one-room school on the corner of Tin and Spruce, two streets from the house.

Deming had been created as a railroad town in 1882 when the Santa Fe Railroad joined the Southern Pacific for the trip west. While Deming's houses reflected the influence of the railroad, they were of a modest variety. But not the rancher's house on Tin Street. The house, which filled the corner lot, featured the architectural details of a style called Adam. The style was an unusual choice considering it was not only a century out of fashion back east, but had never been in vogue in New Mexico (never mind that New Mexico always followed trends a decade or two late).

The simple but classical details certainly complemented the massive adobe walls. But why not Territorial, which had the same effect? That clue is missing. What is known is that from 1780 to about 1820 Adam had been the favorite style of wealthy Americans along the Eastern Seaboard.

The doorway to the Kretek house is classical Adam style. Its transom and sidelights lend a certain delicacy to the surrounding heavy door frame. The center gable, also a feature of the Adam style, crowns the door for added emphasis. To continue this lesson on Adam, note also the style's characteristic shuttered windows and flat lintels.

Mr. and Mrs. Carl Schaber, Barbara Kretek's parents, bought the house from the Birchfield family in the early 1940s. The Birchfields ranched in the Deming area beginning in 1895. Mary Jane Birchfield wrote in her memoirs of living at the "Board and KIL Ranches six years and six months to the day, during which time I never saw a town." Deming was some 27 miles from the ranches and the Birchfields had eight children. Anyone counting days on a ranch surely would have loved a house in town with six bedrooms and two blocks from school.

Cox House

San Augustine Ranch
Circa 1870

Like sixteenth-century sons of Spain, the men who settled Texas following Mexican Independence were fearless adventurers, eager colonists lured to a prickly land. For these Texans, the South was their Spain and their homeland. Like the Spaniards, they carried the old traditions in the marrow of their bones. Texas toughened these southerners, whose sons and daughters grew up independent and proud. The young Texans, inherently restless and fiercely loyal, also displayed a talent for cattle ranching—and trouble. From this generation came men like Oliver Lee, Phelps White, John Chisum and W. W. Cox—all bound for the open range of New Mexico.

W.W. "Bill" Cox and his family migrated to New Mexico in 1888 scouting for a place to establish a sheep ranch. Cox also had taken leave of Texas where the law wanted him for jumping bond after avenging his father's death.

After ranching at three other locations, in 1893 Cox bought the coveted San Augustine Ranch in the Organ Mountains. He first stocked the ranch with sheep but in time replaced them with several thousand head of cattle. By then he controlled 150,000 acres of land including homesteads, railroad lands and mining claims.

Thomas J. Bull, the ranch's first owner of record, also owned a number of enterprises in Las Cruces and Mesilla beginning in 1849. Sometime around 1866 he sold the ranch to Warren T. Shedd, who turned the place into a one-stop entertainment center for prospectors, soldiers and cowboys. The ranch included a small inn, dining hall, hotel and stage stop.

By the time Cox bought the ranch, it had tamed considerably. Cox moved his family into the main house, a *hacienda* with 15 rooms and thick adobe walls surrounding a *placita*. In fortress fashion, the exterior walls had few windows and no outside doors. One room at the north end of the house served as a classroom where Miss Annie Robertson tutored the Coxs' eight children.

The ranch still saw plenty of excitement, however. In 1899 Pat Garrett and a deputy tracking a suspect, found the man washing dishes in Mrs. Cox's kitchen. Just then, a dog belonging to Albert Fall jumped through the window and attacked the lawmen. In the confusion, shots were fired and the alleged fugitive was killed. Cox never forgave Garrett for endangering his family The walls still bear the pockmarks of Garrett's .44. Years later Garrett, who owed Cox money, was shot and killed by Wayne Brazel, a cowboy who worked for Cox. Brazel was later acquitted.

The old charges in Texas still dogged Bill Cox. Finally, he returned to Texas and posted a $5,000 bond. A short time later the Grand Jury of DeWitt County, Texas dismissed all charges. Cox died in 1923, vindicated.

In 1945 the federal government condemned 91 percent of the San Augustine Ranch for military purposes. The Cox family retained the rest, including the ranch house, which today overlooks White Sands Missile Range.

"Why do they call it Thieves' Mountain," I asked...
"It belongs to the Government," Grandfather said.
"Yes, the Government stole it from the cattlemen," Lee said.
"And the cattlemen stole if from the Indians.
And the Indians stole if from the—from the eagles?
From the lion? And before that—?"

Edward Abbey, *Fire on the Mountain*

Bunkhouse

South Spring Ranch, Roswell
Circa 1900

John Chisum left his grandfather's Tennessee plantation at thirteen and moved with his parents to Paris, Texas. There the Chisums prospered and their son, who already carried the nickname "Cow John," perfected his interest in cattle. In 1854 the thirty-year-old Chisum had set up his first cattle operation and by the Civil War his well-stocked ranch was supplying beef to the Confederate army. In the waning days of the war Chisum began looking for new markets. By then, Texas swarmed with ranchers and homesteading farmers competing for the open range. With characteristic foresight, Chisum saw the potential for using New Mexico's free, public domain lands for grazing cattle.

In 1867 Chisum drove a thousand head of cattle into New Mexico to an exchange point on the Pecos River north of Roswell. The next spring, Chisum struck a deal with Charles Goodnight whereby Chisum would drive cattle from Texas to New Mexico. There the herd would take the Goodnight-Loving Trail to markets in Colorado and Kansas. By 1872 Chisum's profits allowed him to buy land north of a campground known as Roswell where trail drivers rested their herds. Two years later he moved his operation to a site on the South Spring River where he had traded 2,400 head of cattle for 40 acres of land and an eight-room adobe called "the square house." By then Chisum had earned a new title—Stock King of New Mexico.

In place of the old square house, he built a new one of adobe and frame, called "the long house." Chisum, who never married, filled his house with an assortment of relatives, servants, and longtime cowhands. Although the house was amply furnished, Chisum preferred to sleep on the floor on a pile of blankets, cowboy style.

Ever in search of new markets, he established a route to Arizona that became known as the Chisum Trail (the famed Chisolm Trail followed a route from Texas to Kansas). The trail threaded through the White Mountains, crossed White Sands and San Augustine Pass, then routed south of Las Cruces where the herd forded the Rio Grande. From there the trail headed straight for Arizona. During 1875 alone more than 10,000 cattle followed the Chisum Trail. However, when Chisum died of cancer in 1884, his ranching know-how died with him.

In 1892 James J. Hagerman bought the South Spring Ranch. Hagerman was a successful entrepreneur who had made money in mining and banking. Of late, he had turned his attention to developing railroad and irrigation projects. His interest in South Spring Ranch stemmed in part from its sheer beauty, plus its proximity to his irrigation projects in the Pecos Valley. Hagerman expanded the ranch to some 6,000 acres and built a three-story English style house grandly called "The Manor." He also built an L-shaped bunkhouse (shown here). The tin-roofed building was made of shiplap wood set on a fieldstone foundation.

Today, Chisum's "long house" is gone, burned who knows when. Hagerman's house has had its top two stories lopped off in the interest of energy conservation. However, the old bunkhouse, original up to its tin roof, sits in the dappled shade of huge cottonwoods. Across the far pasture, where ranch hands are burning ditch weeds, smoke spirals into a cloudless sky.

White House

200 North Lea Avenue, Roswell
1910

Phelps White was satisfied with the bachelor's life until the Christmas he met twenty-year-old Lou Tomlinson in the Roswell post office. Even then, the forty-three-year old rancher was in no hurry to settle down. But when the couple was married three years later, White's change of heart was complete. By 1910 the Whites had four children and a house under construction. Their new home was built in the Prairie style, a thick, squat rendition closely identified with Frank Lloyd Wright's Chicago School of design. One of the few indigenous American styles (Pueblo notwithstanding), Prairie held its popularity a brief ten years before fading from fashion around 1915.

Conveniently, Lou White's father was a Roswell building contractor. Likely, he built his daughter's house from a Wright-inspired plan taken from a pattern book published in the Midwest. The house is solid Midwestern Prairie on the outside—pillared, bricked and hip-roofed. Inside, the house is surprisingly open and airy, Prairie's most endearing features. The interior of the house, while following the Prairie style, leaned toward elegance made possible by White's successful ranching enterprises. For example, in the dining room (shown here), a pair of Tiffany stained glass windows lighten a room lavished with oak trim from wainscot to doorway to ceiling.

White was from an old Mississippi family that had migrated to Gonzales County, Texas, where they farmed cotton on 2,100 acres of rich bottomland. Under the guidance of his uncle George Littlefield, young Phelps White got into the burgeoning cattle business. When he joined his uncle in ranching, he was twenty years old. In 1882, with his uncle's backing, White established his own cattle ranch on 1.5 million acres of New Mexico rangeland, some of which was irrigated from underground wells. White's "windmill ranch" allowed him to weather droughts that struck the eastern plains in the late 1800s. In 1901 White became a partner in Littlefield's 300,000-acre Yellow House Ranch which Littlefield had acquired for $2 an acre.

Then in 1904 White was severely burned when he tried to outflank a prairie fire at the Yellow House Ranch. His cowboy days over, Phelps White returned to Roswell in time for the birth of his first child. He and Lou raised their family in the house they built. After his death in 1934, Lou continued to live in the house until her death in 1972 at the age of ninety-two. The Roswell landmark now houses the Historical Center for Southeast New Mexico.

Cahoon House

612 North Kentucky, Roswell

1928

Roswell was at first only a cattle stop at the juncture of the Hondo and Pecos rivers. Even in 1887 the ranching town consisted of but one house. By the late 1880s, however, the Roswell area was headquarters for several ranching empires, including that of Joseph C. Lea. Lea, who was also a member of the Territorial Legislature, saw the benefits of bringing political power closer to home. The means, he believed, lay in the creation of two new counties. He was right.

In 1889 the legislature carved Eddy and Chaves counties from eastern Lincoln County. Tiny Roswell was named the Chaves County seat and the city began immediate plans for a courthouse on Main Street. By 1890 Roswell could boast of a fire department, a land office, and a new hotel.

That year E.A. Cahoon arrived in Roswell from Albuquerque. Cahoon drove into town in a buckboard flanked by armed guards. In his possession was $50,000 in cash. He went directly to the new Pauly Hotel where in one of the rooms he established Roswell's first bank with himself as cashier.

Cahoon prospered along with Roswell and in 1928 he hired California architect M.C. Parker to design his new home. The Tudor Revival style—dignified yet fashionable—was a wise choice for a banker's house. Tudor was another of those English styles again oddly named (the Tudor line having been passé since the 1500s). Nevertheless Tudor style was at the height of its popularity in the 1920s and 30s in towns like St. Louis and Kansas City. The Cahoon house includes the best of Tudor—fine brickwork, half-timbering, multiple flues with accented brickwork, and steeply pitched gables. Perhaps because of its Midwestern look, the Tudor style is a rarity in New Mexico. In Roswell, however, it looks right at home.

Superintendent's Residence

One Campus Circle, New Mexico Military Institute, Roswell

1931

What creative pleasure the Rapp brothers must have felt each time they designed a building at the New Mexico Military Institute. Over the course of 29 years, Hamilton and William Rapp created buildings that looked like castles, some with towers and turrets, one with an entrance reminiscent of a draw bridge. The architects called their style Scottish Castle, a variation of Military Gothic. By the time the Rapps designed the Superintendent's Residence in 1931, their touch was lighter, just right.

The Superintendent's Residence sits on a broad lawn under huge cottonwoods, its mass in scale with its surroundings. While not overpowering, its most castle-like feature is the entry porch. The porch parapet is crenelated, or indented, for gun (or bow and arrow) placement. The pointed arches are Gothic favorites for churches and castles alike. Bricks the color of butterscotch bring a welcome lightness to the massive structure. The Rapps used this particular type of brick, a Kansas import, on each campus building they designed.

The military institute was the brainchild of Joseph C. Lea, a Roswell rancher and politician. Lea's son had been attending a military school in Fort Worth in part because Roswell had no public school at that time. But when Roswell was named the county seat in 1889, Lea persuaded his son's commandant to start a similar school in Roswell. Goss Military Academy opened in 1891 with 38 students including Lea's son and daughters. However, it soon became evident that the school would need Territorial financial support to remain open. The bill creating the New Mexico Military Institute as a preparatory school and junior college was passed in 1893. The new campus, designed under the master plan of I.H. and William Rapp, opened in 1898 on a 40-acre rise just north of Roswell.

These days Roswell crowds past the campus spreading farther north to a shopping mall at the city limits. The institute, thanks both to its imposing architecture and its reputation, has lost none of its stature. Its former cadets include Peter Hurd, Roger Staubach and Sam Donaldson, plus dozens of generals and admirals. Alumnus Paul Horgan, twice a Pulitzer Prize winner, served as the institute librarian from 1926 to 1944. Today, the institute has some 900 students, nearly 20 per cent of them women.

112

Gesler House

411 West Missouri Avenue, Artesia
1907

The road to Artesia glides over a treeless plain covered with a pale gold stubble that passes for grass. As if to compensate for its harsh, miserly landscape, the earth below stored up measures of water, oil and gas. The town of Artesia, however, is thick with shade trees—a welcome reward for making the trip.

Cottonwood trees grown up beside a spring-fed pond marked the early site for Artesia. Indians, cattlemen and stage drivers all had used the watering hole. The place was known by a succession of names until 1903, after the discovery of artesian water made "Artesia" the obvious choice. By its very name Artesia promised farmers and ranchers a reliable source of irrigation water. Also at that time, the arid lands of the West were open to development under a type of homesteading that fostered irrigated agriculture.

Edward R. Gesler, a farmer from Galesburg, Illinois, quickly realized the connection between artesian irrigation and available land. He arrived in Artesia in 1904 and soon was farming 480 acres just south of town. He also must have been impressed with the concrete "stone" houses he saw in Artesia, for he had one built for himself there in 1907.

Artesia's stone houses turned out to be charming inventions of necessity. (The Romans actually invented concrete, using it most notably to build aqueducts and coliseums. Concrete's strength, in fact, made possible another Roman invention—the arch.) The scarcity of timber and the high cost of shipping made frame and brick construction impractical and expensive in Artesia. The early residents relied instead on two-man stone "factories." The on-site factory consisted of a hand-powered cement mixer and cast-iron molds. Any number of imitation styles was available. Interchangeable face plates on the mold gave the block its distinctive "face," cobblestone or chiseled, for example. Two men operating one block machine could turn out up to 200 blocks a day. Once the house was constructed, the gray concrete stones usually were painted over in chocolate browns, bright whites, or in the case of the Gesler house, sunny yellow.

The Gesler house, like most of Artesia's stone houses, falls into the category known as a Folk Style Queen Anne. The fishscale shingles on the gable make it a Queen Anne, while folk style refers to houses built of local materials by local craftsman. The style depends more on the confines of geography than on the dictates of fashion. In a word, folksy. Also, charming.

Boykin House

400 Sheldon Street, Clovis
1915

Lizzie Boykin's new house on Sheldon Street suited her just fine. Roomy but not fancy—a cross between a farm house and a ranch house. She was pleased, though, that every window had the diamond shape that was so popular with Queen Anne homes. For her husband's sake, she had made sure the house had ample porches. They were both used to fresh air and open spaces, so the porches were nearly a necessity. She was forty-six years old the year her house was built. She would live there the rest of her life.

Lizzie Walters was born on November 22, 1869 near the Ruidoso River nine miles south of Lincoln, the nearest settlement. Her father logged pines in the Capitan Mountains but later sold out to farm and raise livestock south of Lincoln. During her growing-up years, Lizzie viewed the Lincoln County War from the sidelines of her father's ranch. Once when she was visiting children at a neighboring ranch, she watched Billy the Kid, fresh from a jailbreak, file off his shackles and toss them into a stream.

She lived at the family's ranch near Lincoln until 1895 when she married Sid Boykin, a rancher from Portales Springs. Her husband had been in ranching since he was a fifteen-year-old cowboy in Texas. When he finally settled in New Mexico he went into the cattle business for himself at Portales Springs. Later Boykin bought a ranch northwest of the site where the railroad town of Clovis would be established in 1906.

By 1913 Boykin had sold his ranch and taken up cattle trading and the banking business. That year he and Lizzie bought two large lots in Clovis and planned their house. The house was finished in 1915 and Sid and Lizzie settled down to life in town. Sid divided his time between banking and raising prized Herefords, while Lizzie devoted her time to church work. Sid died in 1933. Lizzie lived in the house nearly 20 years more until her death in 1952. They had no children.

Clovis is still a farm and ranch town, although Cannon Air Force Base is a welcome addition to its economy. The Boykin house has had a succession of owners since Lizzie's death. She probably would be happy to know that it's now home to an air force family. The family's curly haired little boy digs in Lizzie's old back yard, collecting rocks and twigs for safekeeping in a bottle.

Cooney/Bamert House

3905 North Highway 85, Las Cruces
Circa 1906

Apaches had prevented outside settlement of the Mesilla Valley since the first Spaniard wandered through the region in 1535. But in January 1843, when New Mexico was under Mexican rule, 33 Mexican colonists established the valley's first permanent settlement. Each family was allotted a *terreño*, or a tract of land for farming. By spring, the colonists had dug an irrigation ditch to their fields. Since Apaches still roamed the area, the farmers worked their fields under the protection of an armed sentry.

By 1916 Thomas F. Cooney owned one of the original *terreños*, which by then totaled 160 acres, including a 44-acre orchard. Cooney's inventory that year tallied 2,950 apple trees, 864 pear trees, and 74 various other trees. Cooney's farm also included a fine double-brick house built about 1906.

The house was built in the Craftsman style. Its craftsman-like quality appealed to those tired of Victorian fussiness and was popular from 1890 to 1920. American architects adopted the English-born style for its middle-class, spreading the word through pattern books offering Craftsman house plans.

The exposed rafter ends and braces of the Cooney house are Craftsman hallmarks. The house's interior, however, shows Craftsman at its best. The pier-like columns (repeated on the sideboard, far right) are not only load-bearing, they also serve as room dividers. The dividers open the rooms to light while maintaining each room's boundaries.

Walter Bamert was born on his father's farm half a mile from the Cooney farm. When he married Ruth Sparks in 1938, they built a house a quarter-mile from the Cooneys. Finally, in 1951 Bamert bought the Cooney place for himself. It took convincing, however,

to get his wife to move into the old farm house. With paint and a little renovation, the house regained its old charm and she was won over.

Once when Bamert and his son were cleaning out an irrigation ditch, they accidently banged their shovels together. The clang rang out across the field. "*No hagas que los Indios te escuchen,*" Bamert told his son. "Don't call out the Indians." The *dicho*, or saying, originated with the valley's first farmers. They worked the fields in silence, taking care lest even the sound of clanking shovels alert the Indians. "*No hagas que los Indios te escuchen,*" they cautioned. Don't call out the Indians.

Apodaca House

13425 Apodaca Road, La Mesa

1945

Sixteenth-century Spain, like brave but misguided Don Quixote, clung too long to its old standards of feudalism. In the end, modern Europe's ideals of industry and commerce left Spain nothing to tender but chivalry and stubborn pride. Spain's place in history, however, would be measured not by its commerce, but its success in converting the New World to its Old World ways. The American Southwest, for example, bears the imprint of Spain's language, its religious zeal—and its architecture.

In the Southwest, the Spanish Colonial Revival style borrowed bits and pieces from Spain's romantic history. The popularity of Spanish Revival, dating from 1915 to the outbreak of World War II, coincided with New Mexico's emergence as a haven for artists and writers whose work romanticized the Southwest.

It wasn't until after the war, however, that José Apodaca, son of a farmer and farmer himself, was able to build his farm house. With the help of two *compadres*, Dick Apodaca and Johnnie Limon, Apodaca built a 5,000 square-foot house from *adobes* made on-site.

The Spanish Revival house was an amazingly sophisticated design considering that Apodaca was thirty and his wife, Gen, was twenty-seven when they built the house. The impact of the overall design is heightened by the contrast of the stark white walls and red tile roof against the shades of greens in the trees beyond and the lawn in front. The house steps up, section-by-section from a low room at one end to the two-story wing at the other. The *torreon*, or watchtower entry, and the large fountain also are Spanish-inspired. In addition to building the house, Apodaca cleared mesquite bushes from 560 acres where he grew cotton, alfalfa, pecans and chile.

Today, Apodaca's daughter Emma Jean Cervantes and her children run the farm, which includes 800 acres of chile and a processing plant. Since the 1970s, the farm has supplied 70 percent of the chile that goes into Louisiana Hot Sauce. Mrs. Cervantes lives in the house her parents built. In 1996 the house was restuccoed—by the sons of her father's *compadres*.

Mabel Dodge Luhan House

240 Morada Lane, Taos

Circa 1920

Turn-of-the-century New Mexico had a long history of disappointed outsiders. In their view New Mexico was a stubborn place, stingy with its resources, and slow to change. Its people were too different, its land too dry. Despite boosts from mining and ranching and railroading, New Mexico in 1900 was a land without recognition. A group of expatriate artists would change all that.

About that time, the art world was giving up still lifes and portrait painting for real-life themes and native settings. Artists, particularly in New York, embraced the new style, but found it increasingly difficult to make a living. The decline in portrait work and the trend toward photoengraving left them out of work and unappreciated. These latter-day colonists found refuge (and less expensive living) in some of the most beautiful settings in America—Carmel-by-the-Sea on the West Coast, Provincetown on the east, and Taos in-between.

By the time Mabel Dodge Luhan came on the scene in 1917, the Taos art colony was flourishing under the nurturing leadership of The Taos Society of Artists. The local population of mainly Hispanics and Indians accepted the Anglo artists into their community with benevolent indifference. Mabel, however, would be their source of gossip for the next two decades.

The much-married Mabel Ganson Evans Dodge Sterne Luhan was born in Buffalo, New York in 1879, the heir to a banking fortune. She used her inheritance to live well and in the company of artists and writers. At her grand villa near Florence, Italy, and later at her New York apartment, she welcomed weekly gatherings of writers, artists and intellectuals, including Gertrude Stein, Pablo Picasso and Henri Matisse. In 1917 she followed her third husband, the artist Maurice Sterne, to Santa Fe, then discovered Taos on her own. She fell in love with the village and promptly decided to make it her home. She also decided to marry Antonio Luhan, a Taos Pueblo Indian who was already married and the father of several children.

In the 1920s she and Tony Luhan began building "the big house," modeled after the multi-storied Taos Pueblo. Within the compound they also built small *adobe* guest houses. The writer D. H. Lawrence described his as a "very smart *adobe* cottage...built in the native style." Although Lawrence was Mabel's most famous guest, she shared her hospitality with a Who's Who of creativity—Thornton Wilder, Georgia O'Keeffe, Mary Austin, Willa Cather, Ansel Adams and Laura Gilpin.

Mabel Dodge Luhan's role as patron of the arts was not so different from that of the artists and writers themselves. Through her patronage and their creativity, the outside world learned to appreciate the Native American culture and value New Mexico for its difference.

Carlos Vierra House

1002 Old Pecos Trail, Santa Fe

1919-1921

By the 1920s the art colony at Santa Fe had carefully unearthed the beauty of New Mexico, shaping it for all the world to see. At the same time, the artists feared they had opened New Mexico to those who might trample its culture underfoot and turn Santa Fe into "an ordinary city." To prevent that, Santa Fe's artists-turned-advocates used their considerable talents to help preserve northern New Mexico's cultural integrity.

Carlos Vierra, a sculptor and a founder of the Santa Fe art colony, took as his personal cause the architectural preservation of Santa Fe's buildings. His greatest feat was the restoration of the Palace of the Governors to its original Pueblo design. Vierra, a California native, had come to Santa Fe in 1904 where he was treated for tuberculosis at the Sunmount Sanatarium. Sunmount, a Pueblo Revival adobe, was designed by New Mexico's earliest architect Hamilton Rapp. The hand-sculpted look of Rapp's design no doubt inspired Vierra in restoring the Governors Palace. Vierra's work, in turn, helped promote the model for what came to be called the Santa Fe Style.

Santa Fe Style was the term coined to promote New Mexico's unique architectural style—namely Pueblo Revival—at the 1914 San Diego Exhibition celebrating the completion of the Panama Canal.

New Mexico in 1912 had finally achieved its quest for statehood and was eager to showcase its Southwest heritage in San Diego. Hamilton and William Rapp were commissioned to design the New Mexico Building for the exhibition.

Meanwhile Vierra continued to guard Santa Fe's landmarks with the zeal he also used to denounce those buildings that strayed from the principles of the Santa Fe Style. Then in 1919, he had the opportunity to build his own house, paid for by art patron Frank Springer with the agreement that Vierra could occupy the house as long as he lived. Springer, a lawyer for the Maxwell Land Grant and for whom the town of Springer was named, also contributed generously to the building of Santa Fe's Museum of Fine Arts. Vierra's house set the trend for other Pueblo Revival houses in Santa Fe. Its classic Pueblo features included massive walls, flat roofs and a setback of successive stories. He rounded corners to softened the massive walls and limited the use of wood to *vigas* and beams over doors and windows.

Vierra lived in the house until his death. The New Mexico Building still exists in San Diego's Balboa Park and the Santa Fe Style still reigns in "the city different."

Belloli-Allen House

1379 Canyon Road, Santa Fe

1935

They say lovers built the house behind these walls. The story of the bittersweet romance between the Italian count and the Boston socialite begins in Mexico, 1929. They might have been introduced, Georgio Belloli to Yolanda Shaw Allen, at a cafe on a crowded plaza. They may have walked together, amid the color and clatter, discussing art. He was a sculptor, she a painter. On the steps of the church they might have talked of its architecture, how different it was from the baroque cathedral in Mexico City. They may have returned there to be married.

Georgio and Yolanda arrived in Santa Fe in 1930 and began building their home on Canyon Road. For five years the newlyweds worked on the house. They shaped the *adobe* with their own hands to give it the sculpted, massive look of the Mexican Colonial style. Mexico's colonial architecture was its own art form, combining the basics of Spanish, Gothic and Moorish design with Indian motifs. Its architecture also was modified to meet the realities of seventeenth-century Mexico. Churches were fortified with heavy doors and thick, windowless walls against the threat of Indian attack. The thick walls also were built to withstand the likelihood of earthquakes.

The Bellolis not only took inspiration from the architecture of Mexico's churches, they also took part of a church itself. It was the practice then—now discouraged—to salvage materials from old churches and buildings and incorporate them into new structures. The Mexican church door served as their entrance gate. The studded gate with its cutout door hints of Moorish ancestry, while the massive pillars have Spanish origins, and the scrolled pediment above the gate borrows from the Aztec period.

When World War II broke out, Georgio (who apparently deserted the Italian navy) joined the U.S. Army. Yolanda stayed on in Santa Fe. When he returned, however, Yolanda found that Georgio was not his old self. Soon he left for Mexico. Although rumor had it that Georgio had remarried in Mexico and had seven children, Yolanda believed he would return one day.

She probably waited for him in the courtyard behind the gate, sitting alone, surrounded by pots of flowers. She may have passed the time remembering Mexico and wondering if Georgio ever walks in the old plaza by the church. Georgio never did return and Yolanda died in the house they built together.

Today, passersby sometimes throw notes over the wall asking to see inside.

Goodwin House

1402 Cerro Gordo, Santa Fe
Circa 1936

This house began life as a barn. But with its setting alongside a narrow, hill-hugging road a mile-and-a-half from the Santa Fe Plaza, plus the added benefit of a spacious interior, it was destined for duty as an art gallery. Dormers, a bay window, French doors, and two sets of small glass-paned windows were added to let in light. Then, with its artistic phase passed, new owners remodeled the gallery into a six-room house.

Even accounting for its barn origins, the house is an unusual style for Santa Fe. Its irregular stonework and steeply pitched roof are features reminiscent of a Dutch Colonial style common to rural eighteenth-century New York. Regardless of its New England profile, however, the house is a New Mexico original. Like its *adobe* counterpart, the house is made from native materials—stones excavated from its surrounding property.

Peter Goodwin, its current owner, first bought the house because it was different from Santa Fe's trademark adobes. He later sold the house but after having discovered he missed living there, he bought it back the next time it went up for sale.

Bushman House

401 West Hill, Gallup
1911

Gallup is a hill town where its east-west streets follow a roller-coaster route and its north-south streets go wherever they please. In 1911 attorney Sam Bushman built a $2,000 house with a view at the top of one of Gallup's hills. The *McKinley County Republican* took note of the house in reporting a visit by Bushman's father from Pennsylvania. "Mr. Bushman is a house painter and decorator and while here will do the decorating and painting of Sam's house, which is nearing completion."

The Bushman house not only was built with a bird's-eye view, it also was built in the latest style. The Craftsman style, a hybrid of English and American parentage, was at its peak popularity in 1911. By then England as well as America had tired of Victorian excess. Plus, designers on both sides of the Atlantic promoted an appreciation for the "craft" of producing furniture and houses. In England, only the wealthy lived in Craftsman houses. But in America, the style was adapted to appeal to the middle class.

The Bushman house was built of sandstone quarried two blocks away. The distance was short but steep, requiring oxen-power for the uphill haul. The putty colored sandstone was used also for the lintels above the windows and the door. Inside, Craftsman features included built-in bookcases flanking the fireplace, and a built-in china cabinet that filled a dining room wall.

Gallup grew uphill from its original site a few blocks north of West Hill Street. There the Rio Puerco followed a level pathway through the sandstone. The Overland Mail took this trail in the 1860s, stopping at a spot shared by an adobe way station and the Blue Goose Saloon. In 1881 the Atlantic & Pacific Railroad laid track through the village in order to ship coal from the nearby mines. The nameless village was also where David W. Gallup, the railroad's paymaster, issued the week's wages. "Going to Gallup's" meant payday. On April 15, 1927 Gallup rejoiced when it found the new national highway, U.S. Route 66, would travel through town on its way from Chicago to Los Angeles. Route 66 became the "road to everywhere." Tourists came to buy Navajo rugs and watch the Indian tribal dances. Dust Bowl refugees straggled through on their way to California. John Wayne and Errol Flynn came to make westerns. Although Interstate 40 has replaced Route 66, the old highway still bustles with tourist and payday traffic.

Davis House

704 Parkland Circle SE, Albuquerque
1928

Albuquerque in the 1920s hummed with the nervous energy of adolescence. It was eager, optimistic, and on the move. With a population that had pushed from 15,000 in 1920 to more than 26,000 in 1930, Albuquerque had become the biggest city in New Mexico's history. In 1922, Albuquerque built the state's first skyscraper—nine stories tall. In 1928, just a year after Charles Lindbergh's solo flight across the Atlantic, Albuquerque boasted having one of the first airfields in the West.

Albuquerque's cultural life also kept tempo with the Jazz Age. Its art colony occupied a charming, inexpensive enclave in Old Town. The KiMo Theater was built in 1927, a one-of-a-kind landmark on Central Avenue. The Albuquerque Little Theater and the Civic Symphony were established in quick succession. In 1927 U.S. Route 66 followed Central Avenue through the city, spurring development of an Art Deco commercial district. At the same time, residential development expanded alongside Route 66 on the East Mesa.

The Parkland Hills subdivision, just blocks from Central Avenue (it has since regained its old designation), was to become a neighborhood of elm-shaded streets, broad lawns and sidewalks. The houses were built with the middle-class in mind, substantial but not pretentious. The Davis house was the subdivision's model home. Hoping to set the tone for the neighborhood, the developers called the Tudor Revival model "The House Beautiful."

Tudor Revival is the warmest of England's medieval architectural offerings. The Davis house especially features the details that give the house its air of cottage coziness. The irregular stonework at the corners, around the windows and on the bulging chimney are meant to give the house an aged, lived-in appearance. The look is akin to allowing *adobe* bricks to show through stucco for authenticity's sake. The false thatched roof is rare even for a Tudor Revival. The clipped ends of the gabled roof make it a "jerkin head" roof, the name bringing to mind a good whack on the forehead.

The charm of "aging" a house is that even today, the Davis house still looks new.

President's House

1901 Roma NE, University of New Mexico, Albuquerque

1930

Albuquerque was a wonder to William George Tight, lately of the University of Chicago and in 1901 the new president of the University of New Mexico. He marveled at its setting, admired its native culture. Evenings he watched the sun's amber light wash across the valley and over to the sandhill campus. He saw how Old Main caught, then absorbed the waning light. The red brick building seemed out of place. Why, he thought, shouldn't a building look like its landscape? He had a plan.

Nearly 13 years before the Santa Fe Style premiered at the San Diego Exposition, Tight and UNM's architect Edward Buxton Christy began exploring nearby Pueblo villages with sketchpad and camera. With the conviction of innocents, Tight and Christy decided to use Pueblo architecture as the model for bringing the campus into harmony with its environment. Albuquerque hardly noticed when in 1904 Tight built a flat-roofed *adobe* heating plant. Students and faculty took delight in Tight's 1906 venture, construction of the first on-campus housing for students. The dormitories—terraced apartments featuring *vigas*, exposed woodwork and roof ladders— were given fanciful Indian names: *Kwataka*, or "man-eaglet" for the men's dormitory and *Hokona*, or "virgin butterfly" for the women's.

Despite its brick facade, Old Main (Hodgin Hall) had never been a sturdy building. Wind whipped at its high, heavy roof and shook its thin walls. When inspectors recommended changing the roof to save the building, Tight was ready with his plan to build a "pueblo university on the mesa." In short work Hodgin Hall's Victorian trappings were swapped for those of Pueblo Revival. The town fathers were horrified by what they called "a revision to the primitive." Tight was blasted on the editorial pages and condemned in Santa Fe. Finally in 1909 he was fired by the Board of Regents. William Tight died a few months later. By then, of course, the movement to define New Mexico's architectural style was just underway. After William Tight's death, students petitioned the Board of Regents for permission to install a memorial marker in his honor. The marker at the entrance to Hodgin Hall reads:

> In Memory of William G. Tight,
> President of this University
> 1901-1909.
> His Monument Stands Before You

In 1927 the Board of Regents formally adopted the Pueblo Revival style for the campus. Architect Miles Brittelle was hired to design the President's house (shown here) in the newly sanctioned style. The house was built in 1930 at a cost of $22,932. University President James Fulton Zimmerman and his wife, Willa, took an active interest in the construction of the house. On moving day, however, the president went fishing, leaving the job to Willa and to Lena Clauve, the Dean of Women.

The house that once was described as being "out with the jackrabbits and rattlesnakes" today lies in the heart of campus. University President Richard Peck and his wife, Donna, welcome thousands of guests to the house each year, who come not only for the hospitality but also for the house itself.

Tingley House

1523 Silver Avenue SE, Albuquerque
1930

Clyde Tingley once had his photograph taken with Charles Lindbergh in front of Lindbergh's airplane. Tingley, stout but smartly dressed, looked every inch the political boss next to the lanky aviator. With typical bravado, Tingley had awarded himself the title of Albuquerque's unofficial mayor and assumed the responsibilities of greeting dignitaries.

Clyde Tingley was born in a log cabin in Ohio and spent his twenties laboring in automobile factories and learning union politics. In Ohio he met Carrier Wooster whose wealth and well-bred background dampened his prospects as her suitor. However, when Carrie was diagnosed with tuberculosis, he followed her to New Mexico where the social climate was more favorable for marriage. The couple (along with her mother) lived at first in a TB cottage in Albuquerque's Huning Highlands neighborhood. There, Tingley's leadership and working-class background easily won him an alderman's seat on the City Commission in 1916, an office he held for 18 years.

By 1930, Tingley had earned begrudging respect for his ability to get things done, namely city ownership of the water utilities system. Under his prodding, the city also planted elm trees, cleaned up trash and regulated billboards. That year he and Carrie hired Charles Lembke to build their house. They wanted a big house, but in light of the Depression and Tingley's political ambitions, they didn't want it to appear too grand. Lembke's solution was to set the house (a Spanish Colonial Revival) high above a finished basement, its height artfully disguised behind a raised entry porch. Upstairs, the Tingleys entertained a lively mix of guests that included university students, shopkeepers, and politicians. Downstairs was Carrie Tingley's famous "toy room" where she collected gifts for hospitalized children. Carrie was a gregarious match for her energetic husband and dressed as vividly as she decorated her house. On one occasion, guests were delighted to see their hostess "dressed like a Christmas tree."

In 1934 Tingley won the first of two terms as governor of New Mexico. During the Depression Tingley used his Washington influence (he was a friend of FDR's) to direct federal aid to New Mexico, particularly to Albuquerque. The city used the funds to build schools, a zoo, the Little Theater, an airport terminal, a fire station, and new fairground buildings. For his part, Tingley's name was affixed to a number of projects, including the Tingley Coliseum.

After the deaths of the Tingleys in the early 1960s their house was converted into a four-unit apartment. The front steps were removed and a parking lot replaced the infamous elm trees and front lawn. The tile fireplace was painted over, indoor-outdoor carpet was glued to the white oak flooring, and particle-board cabinets were installed in the kitchen. Since 1977, however, the house has been slowly restored. The apartments have been removed, the woodwork refinished, and the kitchen restored to its 1930s style. The house also has regained its modest exterior.

Tingley's name resurfaced recently in an *Albuquerque Journal* editorial waxing sentimental about the city's old elm trees. The editor reminded readers that the Siberian Elms were courtesy of Clyde Tingley, "Albuquerque's Johnny Elm seed." The mention would have warmed Tingley's civic heart.

Lujan House

308 15th Street SW, Albuquerque
1936

The Greek Revival origins of New Mexico's Territorial style give it a classic timelessness evident in this Albuquerque Territorial Revival. At first glance, it would be difficult to distinguish the 1930s-era Lujan house from one built in 1880 or one built in 1980. Perhaps it is because the house has all the features of Territorial Revival—crisp, clean lines, an inviting entryway, pedimented windows, chamfered posts, and dentiled brickwork along the roof line.

Designer Richard P. Miller and architect J.B. Burwinkle designed the house for Judge Lujan. It was built in 1936 in Albuquerque's exclusive Huning Castle Addition.

Charles Lembke House

312 Laguna SW, Albuquerque
1937

Charles Lembke, a brick mason's son, practiced his father's trade with the ease that comes from growing up in the business. That self-confidence also allowed him to experiment with a style that took inspiration from the future rather than the past. He would use the style—called Moderne—as the basis for his own home, which itself would become a classic of its type.

The Art Deco Moderne, or Art Deco Streamline, takes its name from a 1925 Paris exhibition that gave artistic expression to machine-age design. The philosophy behind the style was to exploit the advances in technology to create a modern house, a "machine for living." In the form-follows-function manner, the house was stripped of its decorative elements, with emphasis placed instead on its construction materials—concrete, plastic and glass. Symmetry was out, replaced by a desire for harmony and balance. Some of the great movie palaces of the 1920s and 1930s illustrate the harmony of style, down to their Art Deco light fixtures. In the United States, Art Deco Streamline was an industrial designer's dream. Because of its aerodynamic sleekness, designers applied the style to everything from toasters to trains to airport terminals.

The Lembke house features the classic elements of Streamline styling—flat roof, horizontal lines, and rounded corners. The entrance door is hardy noticeable. Instead emphasis is directed toward the end of a long, smooth wall where a curved corner is filled with a three-story wall of glass blocks. Inside, a polished aluminum banister follows a circular stairway along the glass-block wall. The house is also true to style in that it is made from hollow clay tile on a foundation of poured, steel-reinforced concrete. In an innovative evaporative cooling system, the flat roof was flooded with water to cool the house.

Lembke later sold the house and moved into a Ranch style house he built across the street. Over the years, the Art Deco house went through a succession of owners, losing some of its elegance in the process. In 1981 its owners embarked on a three-year project to restore the house to its Art Deco styling. When renovation was completed Charles Lembke and his family were invited to see the results. Lembke also lived to see the restoration of the house where he had grown up—the house his father had built on Walter Street. Charles Lembke died in 1989 at the age of one hundred.

Duarte House

425 West Las Cruces Avenue, Las Cruces
Circa 1910

In the 1880s a savvy group of businessmen invested in farmland bordering Las Cruces on the west. Part of it they donated to the railroad for a right-of-way and depot, then made their profit by subdividing the rest into residential lots. By the time Sixto Duarte built his house in the new subdivision, the railroad had replaced the old wooden depot with one in the railroad's style of choice—California Mission. Duarte's house—solid and square with high ceilings, wood floors, and a breeze-catching central hallway—was also built in the California Mission style. Simple round-arched openings and the low pitched tile roof lent stately beauty to Duarte's big adobe house.

The depot neighborhood settled comfortably into place for the next half century. Following World War II, however, Las Cruces began growing away from the old neighborhood. The railroad was losing business to trucking companies and interstate highways. Then in 1968 the railroad discontinued passenger service to Las Cruces and boarded up the depot. The downtown remodeled its old self in the name of urban renewal, putting on a new face nobody liked. Vagrants began sleeping in the park, wandering the streets. The neighborhood frayed at the edges.

Robert Boswell and Antonya Nelson were living in a one-bedroom condominium when they began looking for a house in 1989. Nelson, who had grown up in an old 26-room house in Kansas, was charmed by the Duarte house because it had big trees and because it was in a neighborhood full of real people. Besides, the four-bedroom house would give them more room for their growing family and more room to write. Boswell and Nelson, who have two small children, share a teaching position in the creative writing department at New Mexico State University. They do their creative writing at home. Boswell, the author of the New York Times best seller *Mystery Ride*, hammers out his fiction in a book-crammed study. Nelson, using a laptop computer, writes from an easy chair in the living room. Her novel *Talking in Bed* was published in 1996.

The house is filled with a comfortable mix of antiques, books, art and music. A huge collage of family snapshots decorates a kitchen wall while bright paintings, Mexican folk art and books spill from room to room. Behind the house an old chile drying shed, 81 feet long, has been converted into a guest house. Guests ranging from the couple's extended family to writers from across the nation have enjoyed the hospitality of the old chile shed.

Today the old Santa Fe depot has a new tile roof imported from St. Louis. Painting and plumbing are next on the to-do list of its new owners, the City of Las Cruces. New street lights brighten Las Cruces Avenue from the depot to the old downtown, which is once again undergoing a face lift. In the neighborhood where Robert Boswell and Antonya Nelson once were warned not to buy—houses now sell in a week.

Hess House

1025 Hess Terrace, Las Cruces
1936

When Fred Hess bought part of an old farm in 1927, he had a specific image in mind for the subdivision he intended to build there. Hess, a real estate developer, took careful interest in the subdivision, partly because it would bear his name, and partly because he planned to live there himself. The houses in Hess Terrace were required to be valued at no less than $2,500 and to be built in Spanish, Pueblo or California Mission style. Hess set the standard with his own house, contracting its design to his friend Gustavus Trost.

Gustavus and Henry Trost were El Paso architects whose designs in Las Cruces included some of its finer homes as well as buildings at New Mexico State University. In 1907, their firm had chosen the Mission style—with a focus on arches, tile roofs, and domed towers—as requisite campus architecture.

In 1936 Gustavus Trost used those same elements (minus the tower) in the house for Fred Hess. Trost designed the house with an abundance of style. Every door and doorway was arched, while walls curved at the ceiling, all lathered in whipped cream plaster. Hardwood floors provided a rich contrast.

The house, the first of 63 residences, was set some 10 feet above and 60 feet back from the horseshoe-shaped street that formed Hess Terrace. The area inside the horseshoe was designated as a park. The subdivision was a "terrace" for good reason. Until flooding in 1865 moved the river a few miles west, the Rio Grande had meandered through land that would become the park. In 1935, a year before Hess built his house, flooding covered the property with water four feet deep. Undaunted, Hess scooped fill dirt from the park and used it to form a terrace around the horseshoe. Houses were built on the terrace, and trees and shrubs were planted in the park. The greenery was later removed, some say because the bushes and trees provided cover for courting couples. According to a less romantic version, the trees were removed to deny shade to vagrants.

Hess Terrace today is a quiet neighborhood of Spanish Pueblo and California Mission houses, integrated by a single brick house trimmed in turquoise. The park, watered from a nearby irrigation ditch, grows nothing higher than a blade of grass.

Dewey House

1401 West Seventeenth Street, Portales
1947-1948

Portales in 1941 was a small college town surrounded by farm and ranch country. When professor Bartlett Dewey and his wife, Evelyn, arrived that year, the campus consisted of a few sturdy red brick buildings. The couple, like newcomers before and since, was captivated by New Mexico's adobe homes—of which Portales had two.

In 1944 they attended a lecture by John Gaw Meem, New Mexico's best known architect at the time. By then Meem already had designed dozens of public and private buildings including the addition to Santa Fe's La Fonda Hotel and the Zimmerman Library at the University of New Mexico. Meem also was the architect to New Mexico's rich and artistic whose grand houses reflected his devotion to the Santa Fe Style.

The Deweys immediately asked Meem to design them an adobe house, which they intended to build with their own hands. In a January 20, 1945 memo Meem noted that the Deweys wanted to decide on a house plan quickly so they could "plant trees this spring...in accordance with their landscaping plan."

The urgency didn't have so much to do with planting trees as it did for Evelyn Dewey's wheat patch. Mrs. Dewey, a farmer's daughter, wanted the wheat planted and harvested in time to make *adobes*. The wheat straw from her garden later was used in making 1,600 *adobe* bricks for the Pueblo Revival style house.

When Meem's design arrived in May, the Deweys were taken aback. The plan called for two stories plus basement at an estimated cost of $19,125. They wrote back expressing surprise at the size of the house and saying they could pay no more than $8,000. Since they were "not in a hurry to build," they told the architect they would consult with him later in the summer. Two years later Meem sent them a second plan for a one-story, one-bedroom house, which he estimated would cost $10,000 to build. "I am sure it will make a nice looking small house," he wrote in closing.

By then the Deweys already had made 1,000 adobes. The house soon became a community project with students, friends and neighbors helping with various phases of construction. It took the entire summer of 1947 to cut and haul pine logs from Cloudcroft for 32 *vigas*. Mrs. Dewey and a home economics professor stripped the bark and varnished the logs. Meem continued to advise them on details, cautioning them, for instance, to dye, not paint, the concrete floor. In November he billed them $535.50 for his architectural services in designing the smaller house.

Dr. Dewey died in 1954 and the house was sold. Evelyn Dewey later married a retired naval officer. In a letter to the house's owners in 1968 she wrote she had lived in 15 houses since leaving Portales but was now comfortably settled on a farm in Nebraska. "I am busy building a garden as always," she wrote. "It is my chief joy."

Hurd-Wyeth House

Sentinel Ranch, San Patricio
Circa 1940

Peter Hurd, the eldest son of a lawyer and grandson of a general, grew up in a big sprawling house in Roswell. Hurd's father, a frail young lawyer with a Boston society background, had come west in the late 1890s for the healing climate. He put down roots in Roswell, married a Gibson-girl beauty, and spent the rest of his long, healthy life engaged in the wool business and natural resources law. He sent his wiry, handsome son to the New Mexico Military Institute in Roswell, then on to West Point to prepare for a military commission.

Henriette Wyeth, the eldest child of a celebrated illustrator, was raised in a house on a hill in Chadds Ford, Pennsylvania. N.C. Wyeth, who came from an old family of Harvard men, was in great demand as an artist, book illustrator and muralist. During the height of his career Wyeth also tutored his remarkably gifted children in a barn-size studio that overlooked the house. Later Henriette, by then a young woman, would take the train into Philadelphia for art classes. On the train home one day, a young man asked Henriette for directions to the Wyeth house where he was to interview as a prospective student. He told her he had once gone to West Point, but had resigned to study art.

Peter Hurd and Henriette Wyeth spent their honeymoon in New Mexico, joyfully holed up in a log cabin in Ruidoso's Upper Canyon. They stayed through the summer and into fall, painting, enjoying the solitude—then returned to Chadds Ford to live under the generous patronage of the Wyeths. By 1932 Peter was gaining national recognition as an artist. He spent time in New Mexico painting a mural at his old school in Roswell. But once back in Pennsylvania he found himself "wishing for more daylight," thinking of New Mexico, yearning for a name of his own. He returned to New Mexico for good. For Henriette, the decision to leave Chadds Ford was wrenching. She stayed behind at first, bound to a loving family whose talent nourished her own. In the end she followed her husband west.

The 40 acres they called Sentinel Ranch lay snug against the foothills of the Capitan Mountains, one dirt road past the village of San Patricio. In anticipation of Henriette's arrival, Peter had cleared out an old three-room ranch house, added indoor plumbing and built a studio for himself. Opposite the California Mission style house, he built another for Henriette. Once she and the children arrived, the house began to take on the polish of the life she left behind—a *sala* finely furnished, flowers in vases, a greenhouse. To these rich tones she added the bright colors of life at the ranch. Evenings on the patio were full of lively talk after the Wyeth fashion, and Mexican folk songs, courtesy of Peter and his guitar. Still, they kept up their disciplined work, painting almost daily.

Over the next 50 years the ranch at San Patricio would become what Chadds Ford had been to an earlier generation—a place of charm and beauty, art and family. Peter Hurd died in 1984. Although Henriette no longer paints, she still lives at the ranch, taking in the north light from her sunroom.

Baker House

1999 Juniper, Los Alamos
1925

Los Alamos has needed no explanation ever since the explosion of the atomic bomb in August 1945. Still, it's jarring to come through the pines of the Pajarito Plateau and find a city that looks like a military base. Anchored at its center, however, is a massive pine lodge that looks quite at home among the pines. At its back are two smaller log buildings. One is now a museum. Until recently, the other was somebody's house.

Dr. Richard D. Baker "the father of Plutonium chemistry" came to Los Alamos in 1943 with a cadre of young scientists whose mission was to beat the Germans in building the atomic bomb. He lived in the log house from 1959 until his death in 1995. In 1943, however, housing at Los Alamos was at a premium and the top scientists received first choice. Sir James Chadwick, the discoverer of the neutron and head of the British Mission to the Manhattan Project, chose the log house. Military officers also lived there for a time.

The house was built in 1925 for the chief mechanic of the Los Alamos Ranch School. The school taught young men of means the skills of outdoor living. Ashley Pond established the Los Alamos Ranch School in 1917 on the Pajarito Plateau, a site he selected for its beauty, its pristine climate, and its isolation. Pond had been a sickly child, the only surviving son of a wealthy Detroit businessman. He had first come West to recuperate from typhoid fever contracted in the Spanish American War. His wife also had spent summers on her grandparents' ranch near Watrous, New Mexico. Although Pond died in 1933, the ranch school continued to flourish. By 1942 it consisted of 54 buildings, including 27 houses. Enrollment had reached its maximum of 44 boys.

In 1942 California physicist J. Robert Oppenheimer was selected to head the Manhattan Project. Oppenheimer had spent time on his family's ranch in the Pecos Mountains and knew that New Mexico's isolation could be key to the success of the project. The ranch school at Los Alamos would be a perfect headquarters. In November, the government bought the 470-acre ranch school and its buildings for $350,000.

By then the war already had affected life at the ranch school. In February 1942 the academic headmaster was called to active duty. Other faculty planned to leave for the military at the end of the term. Airplanes had begun to circle the plateau. Peggy Pond Church, the founder's daughter, lived at the ranch with her husband and two sons. After the ranch sold, civilians, like perspective buyers, were given tours of the ranch school houses. Pond writes that Oppenheimer, "cowboy boots and all," toured her own house, peering into the kitchen and bedrooms before hurrying out the back door.

In the early morning hours of July 16, 1945, Pond awoke from a dream so vivid she recorded it in her journal:

I looked toward the mountains and saw spiralling
streamers of wind forming again and feared that
in them was an irresistible, an invincible force that
was about to destroy the earth.

Bellamah House

11112 Constitution NE, Albuquerque

1955

The war was over. To its liking or not, New Mexico had played an incredible part in its history. The bomb had been built in its pine mountains, detonated on its desert floor. Its villages and reservations had emptied of their young men, gone off to war, come home to cities. Now, New Mexico's military bases and wartime laboratories were being converted for Cold War research and space age rocketry. Albuquerque, at the dynamic center of post-war New Mexico, set itself a furious pace.

In 1942 Albuquerque had 45,000 people. By 1950 the number had jumped to 100,000, then doubled to 200,000 in 1960. Albuquerque's Sandia Laboratories alone employed 10,000 people during the 1950s. At that time Albuquerque had more Ph.D.s per capita than any other city in the United States.

Not only was Albuquerque attracting scientists, it also was filling up with veterans who had seen duty in New Mexico and returned to make it their home. Albuquerque's promise of prosperity also lured young families from New Mexico's rural regions. They all needed a place to live.

Dale Bellamah, real estate developer and master promoter, evicted sheep from the sandy foothills on Albuquerque's East Mesa for the new residents of his planned community. Bellamah's "wife-planned homes" appealed to a waiting list of families. The 850 houses in Princess Jeanne Park (named for his wife) would feature air conditioning, garages, garbage disposals, walk-in closets, and Queen Mary showers. He offered styles ranging from stuccoed neo-Pueblo, to "colorock" brick, to neo-Swiss chalet (shown here). In 1954, a veteran, for example, could buy a $7,850 three-bedroom, one-car garage Pueblo Revival model for nothing down, and $47 a month. A four-bedroom, 1 3/4-bath brick topped out at $10,900. Bellamah's model homes were furnished to showcase labor-saving appliances. One model even featured pink walls and black furniture.

Because Princess Jeanne Park was in the middle of a former sheep pasture, Bellamah planned to attract buyers to the mesa by providing them community conveniences. The park would include a recreation center with a swimming pool, tennis courts, and 300 trees adjacent to a shopping center named Princess Jeanne Plaza. Residents would enter the exclusive community beneath a steel arch Bellamah called the "Gateway to Happiness."

Bellamah's community was such a success that in 1994, the Smithsonian Institution used a model version of a Princess Jeanne house in its Science in American Life exhibit, which celebrated 100 years of science and its effects on everyday life. Although the Gateway to Happiness has since been removed, authentic Bellamah homes still can be viewed from street side in Princess Jeanne Park.

Reynolds House

7 Blueberry Hill Road, Taos
1975

Like a Moroccan mirror-work shawl, this house has a thousand eyes that cannot see. But when the sun hits one just right, a give-away glint hints of life behind its round-eyed stare.

The "eyes" of the Reynolds house are aluminum beer cans (right) set in concrete two cans deep. The inside walls, can for can, look just like the outside walls. This ultimate recycling project is the creative work of Mike Reynolds. His architectural studies at the University of Cincinnati prepared him to design inner city, high density housing. He worked for a time in Austin (a very hip city by Texas standards). Then in 1973, the year of the Arab oil embargo and the "energy crisis," Reynolds moved to Taos and began building houses using solar- and wind-generated sources of energy.

From there it was a small creative leap to designing houses using alternative building materials. His training in low-cost urban design helped form his philosophy toward home building. He believed a design should make use of simple methods and inexpensive materials to allow people to build their own homes.

His first houses, like the one shown here, were built entirely of aluminum cans. Others were made from beer bottles whose necks faced outside where the wind whistled across their tops. When aluminum recycling cut into his supply of free cans, Reynolds turned to yet another source for discards. These days Reynolds designs "earthships"—houses built from old tires. His earthship books, like the nineteenth-century pattern books before them, provide inexpensive designs for do-it-yourself home builders.

Wheeler House

939 Kit Carson Road, Taos

1989

The art colonies at Santa Fe and Taos thinned to near extinction in the 1940s. Santa Fe counted only two art galleries in 1945, while in Taos artists even as well known as Gustauv Baumann were having trouble making ends meet. By the 1950s, New Mexico had begun to regain its creative energy. The dynamics, however, differed from those of the old art colonies. First, the new breed of artist was an individualist rather than a colonist. Second, those who bought art likely were Texans who had come to ski, then left with a painting or two. Patrons continued their crucial role in fostering the arts. By the late 1980s Santa Fe had nearly 200 art galleries. In Taos, R.C. Gorman was meeting ends quite well selling his paintings of blanket-draped Navajo women.

Thom Wheeler is typical of the modern Taos artist in that Taos has no typical artists. He's a talented tin sculptor, a relentless house-builder, and a can-do Texan. When he first came to Taos he lived in a Victorian house and in 1989 began building a foundry and studio.

Four years and 38,000 *adobe* bricks later he found himself with an adobe "castle," which became his home as well as his studio. His Pueblo Revival castle includes Moorish influences (pointed arched windows on the second floor), and a collection of antique "findings." The entry to the bathroom, for example, is framed with columns from a funeral home, and flanked by a stuffed rooster, a tin mask and two cowboy hats.

Next door to the castle is Wheeler's latest work-in-progress—a three-story Victorian barn. The barn, which will serve as his carpenter shop, is being built from pieces of his Victorian house in Houston. When the new owners demolished the house to build a parking lot, Wheeler salvaged the materials and brought them to Taos for his barn.

Maybe not in Santa Fe, but in Taos a Victorian barn seems a perfect complement to an adobe castle.

Healy House

Tepee, Arroyo Hondo
1994

The communal spirit of the early Taos and Santa Fe artists wandered adrift for a generation or two before finding its place again in the "flower children" of the 1960s. Taos, which had nurtured artists of that earlier time, became common ground once more. This generation, however, was devoted not so much to art as it was the communal experience.

A dozen miles north of Taos artisan "hippies" settled near Arroyo Hondo where they established communes with names like New Buffalo, Morning Star and Reality Construction. A century earlier Arroyo Hondo had been Penitente land where from the village church Padre Martinez practiced his own brand of rebellion. Today, Arroyo Hondo shares the Taos Valley with the Taos Pueblo and the ruins of ancient villages.

The valley's newest residents, like others before them, both changed and were changed by this historical landscape. John Nichols, for instance, came to Taos in 1969 and stayed to chronicle the valley's fight for water in *The Milagro Beanfield War*. He lives here still. That year Dennis Hopper spent a few weeks in Taos making *Easy Rider* and soon returned to buy Mabel Dodge Luhan's old house. He later left the scene, but his brother David, who had restored the Luhan house, stayed on.

David Hopper has spent nearly three decades restoring old adobe houses and building new ones. During this time he and a group of artist-craftsmen under the name Flowering Tree collectively operated an art gallery and built houses together. Today, Flowering Tree still builds houses. Besides Hopper, its members include a jeweler from a long-time Arroyo Hondo family, a silversmith who was an original member of the New Buffalo commune, a silversmith who also is a *santero*, and a sculptor who leads a salsa band.

Ed Healy first came to Taos 20 years ago where he later met Taos native Trudy Knox at her art gallery. Knox, whose great-grandfather painted the church altars at Las Trampas, is a musician and poet. Healy's family has a long tradition of supporting the arts. For instance, M.A. Healy Foundation grants have been used to purchase art work for the Harwood Museum in Taos, and to fund the restoration of churches in Arroyo Seco and Arroyo Hondo.

When Ed and Trudy decided to build a house in Arroyo Hondo, they chose Flowering Tree, builders whose philosophy matched their own. As expected, the house followed the creative spirit of its owners and its builders. After Healy drew up the plans, Hopper sited the house on the North Star. As a result at the fall and spring equinox, the setting sun lines up with the diamond-shaped windows in the master bedroom. In a departure from the flat-roofed *adobe* style, theirs became a house of thirteen gables. Inside the artisans created ceilings patterned with cedar and spruce, walls with stone mosaics, and an *adobe banco* inlaid with tile.

Ed and Trudy Healy moved into the house September 17, 1994, on the night of their wedding. They held the reception at their new house where some 500 guests feasted on roast buffalo and danced the Taos Fandango.

Kellahin House

706 Gonzales Road, Santa Fe
1972

The pond's the thing. Jim and Linda Kellahin rented a backhoe and dug it themselves, completing it 298 days over schedule in what they call "Santa Fe time." Although Jim is from Santa Fe and Linda is from Los Angeles, the inspiration for the pond came about after a two-year stint living in the Philippines. When they returned to their home in Santa Fe, they found they missed the Philippine water gardens. Their water garden, six feet at its deepest, is stocked with Japanese Koi, a fish from the carp family. The pond's resident Koi come in a variety of colors and personalities. A small side pond serves as a nursery and infirmary, depending upon the need.

Unlike the pedigreed fish, the Kellahin house is of mixed lineage. The original portion of the house contains hints of Territorial style. The frame of its large picture window, for example, is slightly pedimented and bricks line the flat roof. The two-story addition retained the Territorial style brick courses at the roof line but borrowed from the Pueblo Revival style for the portal with its corbel and post features. Linda Kellahin sheepishly points out these architectural inconsistencies, but in good humor admits they devoted their attention mostly to building the pond.

Bieri House

43 Rock Ridge Drive, Albuquerque

1988

Parallel lines beneath a broken ridge, glass reflecting rock, soft pink against conglomerate gray. Harmony. And a view.

John Michael and Rita Bieri had both in mind when they asked Suzanne and David Williams to design their home. The result is an Art Deco Moderne house that complements its Sandia Mountain setting and takes in the panorama below.

Behind a bush, Kokopelli, the humped back flute player, practices his seductive song, dancing to his own tune.

Euline/Komadina House

475 Camino Corrales del Norte, Corrales
1986

The Rio Grande once served to isolate Corrales from the busy world beyond. A Spanish land grant opened the lands west of the river to European settlement in 1710. By 1776 some 200 residents lived in adjacent farming communities known as Upper Corrales and Lower Corrales. A hundred years later Corrales listed a population of 687. Throughout the Spanish and Territorial periods, Corrales remained off the major trade routes, its residents content with farming and raising livestock.

From the turn of the century until World War II, Corrales was known for its vineyards and apple orchards. During that time, healthseekers and others drawn to the Southwest began arriving in Albuquerque, pushing up its population, and spilling ever so slightly over into Corrales. Then in 1957 a new bridge was built over the Rio Grande. Although the bridge ended Corrales' splendid isolation, its rural character held. However, on the sandy mesa at its western edge, developers were soon at work creating the town of Rio Rancho, and promoting it to Sunbelt retirees.

In 1986 Paula Euline, an heiress of the Schlitz family, built an estate along the Rio Grande where huge cottonwoods provide a lush foreground for the Sandia Mountains that loom beyond. She chose Corrales because it was both tranquil and accessible. There she built a 30-acre breeding and training facility for thoroughbred horses as well as a 7,000-square-foot Pueblo Revival home for herself. The 36-foot living room (opposite) features *vigas* as large as three feet in diameter. Massive timbers in the master bedroom also lend support to a helicopter landing pad on the roof.

Dr. Steve and Penny Komadina bought the estate in 1990 and live in the main house. The horse facility, however, has been converted into a petting zoo of sorts. Among the Komadina's menagerie are water buffalo, monkeys, camels, llamas, miniature horses and pot-bellied pigs. Apartments that once housed the training staff are now bed and breakfast facilities, while a large office/meeting area serves functions ranging from weddings, to retreats, to family reunions.

Today, the view to the east is still pastoral and peaceful. But at the estate's southern boundary, rush-hour traffic takes the hill to Rio Rancho where some 4,200 people work at Intel Corp., the world's largest maker of computer chips. In the summer of 1996, New Mexico's largest shopping mall opened a mile south of Corrales.

Forrest House

1306 West Riverside Drive, Carlsbad
1984

The Pecos River runs through Bob and Barbara Forrest's back yard, serving as a picturesque reminder of Carlsbad's good fortune in the midst of an otherwise rough country.

The Pecos is a home-grown river, spawned from snowmelt high in the Sangre de Cristo Mountains northeast of Santa Fe. Once it leaves mountain country, the Pecos heads south along the prairie grass edge of the High Plains. The river arrives at Roswell sapped of its vitality, briny and heavy with silt. There, however, the Pecos begins its revival, replenished by groundwater with origins in the mountains to the west. Downstream at Carlsbad the Pecos arrives newly springfed, reflecting the color of the sky.

In the 1880s Charles B. Eddy, a former New Yorker and confirmed capitalist, was deep in the cattle business in New Mexico. Eddy believed the combination of river and railroad development would transform the Pecos Valley into a paradise. A first step in the transformation was the 1888 dedication of a townsite (named for Eddy) on the Pecos. By then, he and Pat Garrett, who was looking to make a name for himself as a businessman, formed an enthusiastic partnership to develop an irrigation system called the Carlsbad Project. The system, including construction of two dams, was completed in 1893. Their achievement was short lived when floods washed out the dams that year and again in 1904. Despite considerable investment, including a $40,000 infusion from James Hagerman, the company finally folded. As it happened, the government was just then into the dam-building business. In 1907 the U.S. Bureau of Reclamation took the Carlsbad Project under its federal wing and rebuilt the dams. By then the citizens of Eddy had changed its name to Carlsbad (a name borrowed from a health spa in Czechoslovakia) to promote its mineral springs.

Today, the dams on the Pecos River above Carlsbad divert water for some 25,000 acres of irrigated cropland, plus provide flood control for the entire valley. Although the river has always provided recreation as a side-benefit, in 1984 it took center stage. That year the city embarked on a Main Street America program to expand its river park. Under the leadership of Bob Forrest, who was then mayor, development on the river included building a walking path, converting an abandoned amusement park into a mini-convention area, and turning an old power plant into a youth center. One of the city's most popular attractions has become "Christmas on the Pecos," boat rides on the river to view the lighted holiday displays of Carlsbad's riverside homes, including the Forrests' stucco Ranch style house.

In summer the view from the Forrests' back yard (shown here) takes in a river busy with boaters and jet skiers. Farther downstream children splash in a roped off section of the river, while a lone picnicker watches from the shade of a downy cottonwood. Though it's not the paradise of Charles Eddy's vision, the river town that once shared his name holds riches he never imagined.

Hubbard House

100 Willie Horton Drive, Ruidoso
1990

John Chisum's trail drivers rested thirsty herds along the Rio Ruidoso in the 1870s. By 1885 the cattle stop had become a small trading center complete with store, post office and blacksmith shop. Ruidoso has been cowboy country ever since.

In the 1940s ranchers from Texas, Oklahoma and New Mexico congregated at a grassy meadow outside Ruidoso to race their fastest horses. Wagering at the "track," an old cow pasture set up with rickety bleachers, reached as high as $50,000 for a single race. About that time, wide-open illegal gambling hit New Mexico like a fever. Ruidoso, caught in the frenzy, added slot machines and roulette wheels for gamblers who preferred indoor sports. The state shut down illegal gambling in the late 1940s, but under law did allow parimutuel horse racing. In 1947 near the old meadow, quarter-horses raced on a new—and legal—racetrack. Ruidoso Downs in 1959 featured the world's first $1 million horse race.

Fort Worth businessman R.D. Hubbard bought the track in 1988, pouring more than $3 million into improvements. In addition, Hubbard and his wife, Joan Dale, were instrumental in building the Museum of the Horse at Ruidoso Downs. The museum, as fine as any, pays tribute to western life through its exhibits, art work and collections.

In Ruidoso Hubbard built a golf course on land that had been the old Ruidoso Airport. At its edge he built his house, in some ways also a monument to the horse. The house, built with the stark simplicity of the International style, serves as outdoor exhibit space. An abstract stained glass window "hangs" on its east wall, which in turn serves as the backdrop for a pair of bronze horses splashing in a fountain. A stallion rears from the water, twisting toward the morning sun—showing off.

Leake House

James Dean Drive, Columbus
1990

Without clouds to deflect its aim, the winter sun throws hard shadows against an *adobe* wall. This is not the painterly light of New Mexico's north country, but Chihuahuan light, the undimmed bright of the desert south. Nancy Leake, a sculptor from Wisconsin, built this house three miles from the Mexican border. Her sense of light and dark, contrast and shadow served her well in a landscape lacking the shade of a single tree. Alongside the arroyo she fashioned a pair of *adobe* arm chairs and several *adobe* stools. The friendly companion of current owner Helena Myers finds that an "overstuffed" chair makes a comfortable spot on a winter's day in the desert (left).

Jacobs-Ritter House

3610 Southwind Road, Las Cruces
1972

Aqui la Puerta es Corazón Siempre Abjerto.
Here, the door, like the heart, is always open.

Even if the plaque by the door didn't announce it, the house Kent Jacobs and Sallie Ritter built as newlyweds practically beams with hospitality. Kent and Sallie both grew up in the Mesilla Valley. Kent's father founded the music department at New Mexico State University in 1930, while Sallie's family dates back five generations in New Mexico. They didn't meet, however, until Sallie was back from art studies in Colorado by way of the University of Rome and Edinburgh College. By then Kent was home from medical school and already practicing dermatology in Las Cruces.

After their marriage they bought property at the edge of a farm and began building their "pay-as-you-go" house. They based the design on the Mexican Colonial mansions in Alamos, an eighteenth-century silver mining town in Sonora, Mexico. The town had become their favorite and on visits there Sallie had sketched the old mansions, noting especially their carved *mudéjar*, or Moorish, pillars. Sallie sketched a water color of each room in the house to guide workmen during construction. Kent's creative contribution was a foam-core model of the entire house, which in reality would be *adobe* with Mexican stone accents, including *mudéjar* pillars. Carved stone blocks would be used to add texture to the double entry (shown in cover photograph), just as *mudéjar* pillars would be used to add emphasis to the *portal* at the rear of the house.

During construction, Kent and Sallie hauled water to the gangly poplar trees they had planted along the long drive to their house. In 1972 the house was finished and the trees had settled in. A line of leafless poplars, reddened at sunset, later would be subjects in one of Sallie's paintings.

The house, which since has been enlarged to include a writing study for Kent and a pool house for entertaining, is an art collector's dream. In the living room alone (opposite) are the famous black pots made by Maria Martinez, a Tarahumara water jug, and a painting of a woman by Siqueros. In the dining room, the painting of three figures is by Las Cruces artist Spencer Fidler. Sallie's own paintings—landscapes in themes of sunset, mist, snow and frost—hang in galleries in Aspen, Santa Fe and Las Cruces.

These days Sallie paints in her downstairs studio, while Kent (who still maintains an active medical practice), writes novels in his upstairs study. Within a month of each other recently, Sally's exhibition of paintings titled *Lightscapes* opened in Santa Fe, while Kent's first novel, a spy thriller titled *Breckkan* made its debut in Las Cruces.

Hanssen House

1520 Vista del Valle, Las Cruces

1989

With just the right perspective, this house looks like a desert planting dish. Soaptree yucca in one corner, purple sage crowding below. Ocotillo in spiny profile. Tufts of Spanish broom, and prickly pear everywhere. The Hanssen house, through the artful work of architect Ron Nims, passes the test of Contemporary Southwest style—it looks at home in its landscape. He also designed the house to take in the view. Because owners Stan and Jeanne Hanssen, who had just spent 14 years in Ireland, wanted the feeling of wide-open spaces, they set the house at the edge of the west mesa. To the west, the house faces the desert. On the east, however, it overlooks the Mesilla Valley where the Rio Grande's silty path cuts through fields of chile and alfalfa.

Waters House

7027 Raasaf Circle, Las Cruces
1996

Bette Waters' dream house sits on the side of a mesa above a thicket of honey mesquite. From that thorny perch, however, is a spectacular view of the river valley and the mountains beyond. Besides, the house is exactly what Waters wanted—something solar, something sturdy, and something in a style that fit its environment.

Although the Waters house has the soft doeskin look of traditional adobe, it is built of rammed earth, a mixture of earth and cement. Rammed earth construction involves using plywood forms to create hollow walls which are then filled with a mixture of moist earth and cement, with cement as the stabilizing ingredient. The mixture is then pounded, or "rammed," using a compressor-powered tamper, to form a tightly compacted wall. Once the fill has been compacted, the form is removed to reveal a solid wall one to two feet thick. The process is quick. For example, a wall 4 feet high and 10 feet long takes about half an hour to pour and compact. The high ratio of cement to earth gives rammed earth its durability.

Rammed-earth walls, known as *pisé* in many French-speaking countries, is a construction method dating from prehistoric times. It is believed to have evolved from "puddled" wall construction, a technique where dough-like mud is laid in courses without benefit of wooden forms. Because each layer had to dry before the next course could be applied, construction of one 12-inch thick wall, could take several months. Puddled *adobe*, sometimes called "coursed" adobe, is still used in many part of the world.

However, in those societies with the skills and tools to create forms, rammed earth became a more viable construction method. Rammed earth has been widely used in the arid climates of Australia and North Africa as well as in humid countries such as France. In the United States, rammed-earth buildings, dating from the mid-1800s, also can be found in places like South Carolina and New York.

Today, rammed earth seems to have regained its place among the list of revived building methods. Like its *adobe* counterpart, it is an efficient "thermal moderator." The massing of its walls collects and re-radiates the warmth of the sun in winter, while its earthen qualities retain their cool in summer. The Waters house, a passive solar design, has south-facing windows that allow the winter sun to warm the concrete floors inside. In summer, the hill to the west and a solid west wall block the sun's heat.

Bette Waters' dream house one day will be her retirement home. If rammed earth lives up to its reputation, the house will last her a long, long, long time.

Chavez House

1600 Elder Street, Las Cruces
1993

When the ancestors of the Acomas ceased their wanderings, lore has it that the "mother of all Indians" led them to Acoma Pueblo. On that high mesa she showed them how to build houses using sticks and stones and earth. In fact, Pueblo women by virtue of their pottery-making skills were adept at building and plastering *adobe* houses. By tradition, they also owned them.

Esther Chavez may not have known this legend when she took up hammer and saw, but she followed their tradition just the same. With a year's worth of "sweat hours" and the labor of family and friends, she and her daughters have a house of their own. The Chavez house was made possible through Habitat for Humanity.

Habitat for Humanity was the inspiration of Millard Fuller, a millionaire lawyer from Alabama. As volunteers, Fuller and his family had helped build homes for poor people in Georgia and in Africa. In 1976, Fuller founded Habitat for Humanity with the belief that the community, in partnership with needy families, could build decent, affordable housing. Since its founding, Habitat for Humanity has built some 40,000 houses around the world.

Chavez, a single mother, earned eligibility for her own home first by putting in 100 hours of work helping build other Habitat houses. She began with simple cleaning chores, then learned to frame and sheetrock. She spent another 400 hours working on her own three-bedroom, one-bath home of frame and wood siding construction. During that time her uncle helped sheetrock, her sister painted, and a friend installed the insulation. Her mother and daughters helped with sweeping, cleaning, and later the landscaping. It took Chavez a year of nights, weekends, and vacation time from her job to complete the house. Chavez still has responsibility for the mortgage. In Las Cruces, for example, the interest-free mortgage on a Habitat home averages from $200 to $250 a month for 20 to 25 years.

Chavez has made good use of the skills she gained from her Habitat work. She does her own home repairs and services her own air conditioner. Her younger daughters, ages twelve and fourteen, also have pride in the home they helped build. The first night in their new home, they ate dinner sitting on the floor. Chavez says her daughter looked around, then smiled and said, "This is home."

Acknowledgements

This book would not have been possible without the generous cooperation of the owners of the homes who shared their personal stories as well as their private papers. Special thanks goes to Jim and Ann Carson who introduced me to the importance of historic preservation and whose own Albuquerque neighborhood demonstrates the rewards of volunteer efforts such as theirs. Mary Davis, former planner for historic preservation for the City of Albuquerque, was a valuable resource in the early stages of the project. Dr. Mary Ann Anders, architectural historian for the New Mexico Historic Preservation Division in Santa Fe, cheerfully answered requests for information from beginning to end.

Staffs at local, state and federal agencies answered questions, supplied background information, and led me to published sources. Theresa M. Hanley, an archeologist with the Bureau of Land Management, proved an important source of information on Lake Valley. New Mexico Press Women members from throughout the state were an incredible network for ideas, contacts and sources of information. Their moral support was equally valuable. Ron Balmer, executive director of the Carlsbad Chamber of Commerce, was especially helpful in suggesting sources on the Pecos River as was Cathy Ortega Klett, reports coordinator for the New Mexico Water Resources Research Institute. Gary Esslinger, manager of the Elephant Butte Irrigation District and a third-generation farmer in the Mesilla Valley, helped me scout farm houses.

Architects Rem Alley, Ted Shelton, Ron Nims and Tomás Mendez, all of Las Cruces, were ready sources of advice and information. The kind assistance of architect Kory Baker gave me a starting place in exploring Albuquerque's modern architecture.

Realtors provided additional assistance. In Las Cruces Elaine Szalay, a broker at Metro 100 who specializes in historic homes, generously loaned her background files. Weyland Burke, a broker with Re/Max, provided much-needed direction on a rainy day in Ruidoso, while Alison Tinsley, with Barker Realty, proved a pleasant guide and lunch companion in Santa Fe.

Local museums were as helpful as they were interesting. Special thanks goes to the staffs at the Aztec Museum, the Silver City Museum, the Artesia Museum and Art Center, the Deming Luna Mimbres Museum, the Columbus Historical Museum, the Kit Carson Historical Museums in Taos, the Branigan Cultural Center in Las Cruces, the Lincoln County Heritage Trust, the Los Alamos Historical Museum, and the Historical Center for Southeast New Mexico at Roswell. I thank also local historian Don McAlavy who shared his unpublished research on Clovis, as well as Roger Walker for his information on Alamogordo's historic homes.

As always, librarians helped make my work easier. My appreciation goes to the staffs at the Ratón Public Library and the Carlsbad Public Library. The architectural archives at the University of New Mexico and the Rio Grande Historical Collections at New Mexico State University were invaluable. Special thanks to Cheryl Wilson, special collections at NMSU, for helping track down maps. Steve Pasternak, NMSU's journalism department head, provided important guidance on the legalities of photographing houses.

I am indebted to those who gave of their time and expertise to review the manuscript. Carole Larson is the author of *Forgotten Frontier*, a history of southeastern New Mexico. Dr. John P. Wilson's long list of published history includes *Merchants, Guns and Money*, a history of the Lincoln County Wars. Dr. Spencer Wilson is a retired professor of history at New Mexico Tech and member of the editorial board of the Historical Society of New Mexico. Susan Berry, director of the Silver City Museum, is co-author of *Made to Last*, an architectural history of Silver City. John Grassham is the curator of history at the Albuquerque Museum and past president of the Historical Society of New Mexico. Ed Boles is a planner with the Historic Preservation Program for the City of Albuquerque. I was fortunate also for the editorial expertise of Marilyn Haddrill, a career journalist as well as published fiction author. Darlene Reeves, as always, was a most careful proofreader. Thanks also to photographer Scott Vance for his advice and assistance and to Russell Bamert for the loan of his photographic equipment.

I was accompanied in this trek by two very dear people. The first is Pamela Porter—photographer, writer and friend. Her professional poise and determination saw us through many an adventure. The second is my husband, Jim Harris. As my critic, he kept me honest. As my scheduler, he kept me on track.

Glossary

ADOBE: Brick of sun-dried earth and straw; a structure made with adobe bricks.

ASHLAR: Stonework of square or rectangular stones, usually laid in a regular pattern and smooth faced.

BALUSTRADE: A row of short, column-like supports topped by a rail, with or without a base.

BANCO: A low adobe bench attached to a wall

BOARD AND BATTEN: Frame construction of vertical boards, with their joints covered by narrow wood strips called battens.

BRACKET: A support element under eaves, shelves or other overhangs, often more decorative than functional.

BUTTRESS: A projecting structure of masonry or wood to support or stabilize a wall or building.

CANALE: A drain spout from a roof.

CANTILEVER: A projecting beam anchored to a wall to support a balcony.

CHAMFERED: Cut off corners or edges; usually applies to posts but also can apply to a corner of a building.

CLERESTORY: A windowed wall or construction used for light and ventilation.

CORBEL: A projecting piece supporting a beam; similar to a bracket.

CORNICE: The projecting horizontal piece that crowns an architectural composition.

COURSED ADOBE: A building method where mud is layered by hand in bands to form a wall; also called puddled adobe.

DENTIL: A series of small blocks that project like teeth.

DORMER: A vertically set window on a sloping roof; the roof with such a window.

EAVES: The projecting overhang at the lower edge of a roof.

FOGON: A corner-set fireplace.

FANLIGHT: A semicircular or fan-shaped window with radiating pieces or tracery set over a door or window.

FLUTED: Having regularly spaced vertical, parallel grooves or "flutes," as on the shaft of a column, pilaster or other surface.

GABLE: The triangular portion of an end wall between the slopes of the roof and under the roof ridge; a roof with such ends.

GAMBREL: A ridged roof with two slopes on each side, lower slope having the steepest pitch.

HACIENDA: A self-sufficient rural estate, farm or ranch; the house of the owner; a low sprawling house with projecting roof and wide porches.

HALF-TIMBERED: A heavy wood-braced frame filled in with brick, or stone.

HIP ROOF: A roof with four uniformly pitched sides.

JERKIN HEAD: A gabled roof with the ends partially clipped at an angle.

LIGHTS: Windows.

MANSARD ROOF: A roof whose lower pitch is almost vertical, creating a full attic story, and whose upper pitch has a low slope.

MORADA: A chapel of the Penitentes, a brotherhood of lay Catholic men.

NICHO: A niche cut into an adobe wall for decorative purposes.

ORATORIO: A private chapel.

PALLADIAN WINDOW: A set of window openings with a large arched central window with flanking rectangular side windows.

PARAPET: A raised wall above a roof line.

PEDIMENT: A triangular crowning element used over doors, windows and niches.

PILASTER: A shallow, half-column built against the wall of a building.

PLACITA: A small plaza serving a complex of buildings or located in the center of a home.

PLAZA: A public square.

PORTAL: A long porch or portico with roof supported by vertical posts and corbels.

PORTICO: A featured entrance porch, usually with a crowning roof supported by columns.

QUOIN: Stone or brick used to accentuate the corners of a building.

RAMMED EARTH: A building method where a mix of mud and cement is compacted into a wooden form to make a wall.

SALA: A formal living area.

SIDELIGHTS: Narrow fixed sash lights flanking a door.

SPINDLE: A turned wooden element, often used in screens, stair railings and porch trim.

STUCCO: Waterproof plaster for exterior walls, often with a finish of small pebbles.

TRANSOM: A small window directly over a door or window, usually hinged.

TURRET: A small, slender tower usually at the corner of a building, often containing circular stairs.

VERANDA: A large roofed porch extending around two or more sides of a house.

VIGA: A ceiling beam.

WAINSCOT: Wood paneling, usually on the lower part of a wall.

ZAGUAN: A roofed space joining separate buildings or rooms, often wide enough for vehicles or animals; an entryway to a placita.

Suggested Readings

The readers of this book are like browsers at an open house, looking at history on a leisurely afternoon. Some, however, may want to study the blueprints, the books used as the foundation for *Houses in Time*. Those books are listed here for further reading. Any in depth study should begin with *A Selected Bibliography of New Mexico History*, compiled by Jon Hunner. The bibliography, divided by subject, lists books by era and subject.

Two architectural guides are useful primers on American architecture: *House Styles in America: The Old-House Journal Guide to the Architecture of American Homes* by James C. Massey and Shirley Maxwell, and Virginia and Lee McAlester's *A Field Guide to American Houses*. *What Style Is It?: A Guide to American Architecture* by John C. Poppeliers, S. Allen Chambers, Jr. and Nancy B. Schwartz is a handy pocket guide.

New Mexico's Pueblo architecture is covered in a wealth of books including Bainbridge Bunting's *Early Architecture in New Mexico*, *Of Earth and Timbers Made: New Mexico Architecture* and *Taos Adobes: Spanish Colonial and Territorial Architecture of the Taos Valley*. *Navajo Architecture* by Stephen Jett and Virginia E. Spencer, and *Navajo Material Culture* by Clyde Kluckhohn, W.W. Hill and Lucy Wales Kluckhohn cover a lesser-known area of Native American architecture. Jerome Iowa's *Ageless Adobe: History and Preservation in Southwestern Architecture*, *Old Santa Fe Today*, edited by Sylvia Glidden Loomis, and *Old Houses of New Mexico and the People Who Built Them* also are important studies in New Mexico architecture. No listing of architectural readings would be complete without V.B. Price's thought-provoking book on modern Albuquerque, *A City at the End of the World*.

Books resulting from architectural surveys provide looks at both local architecture and local history. Those include *Built to Last: An Architectural History of Silver City, New Mexico* by Susan Berry and Sharman Apt Russell, *Treasures of History: Historic Buildings in Chaves County 1870-1942*, edited by William E. Gibbs, *The Las Cruces Historic Buildings Survey*, edited by Anne E. Kapp and Guylyn Nusom, and *The Territorial History of Socorro, New Mexico* by Bruce Ashcroft.

The works of the region's pioneering architects are covered in *Creator of the Santa Fe Style: Isaac Hamilton Rapp, Architect* by Carl D. Sheppard, *John Gaw Meem: Southwest Architect* by Bainbridge Bunting, and *Henry C. Trost: Architect of the Southwest* by Lloyd and June-Marie F. Engelbrecht.

Marc Simmons provides an overview of New Mexico history in *New Mexico: An Interpretive History*, while Francis L. and Roberta B. Fugate trip around the state with their *Roadside History of New Mexico*. *New Mexico Past and Present: A Historical Reader* edited by Richard N. Ellis covers important topics in New Mexico's history. Contrasting to these contemporary, fast-paced histories is Erna Fergusson's lively 1951 narrative *New Mexico: A Pageant of Three Peoples*.

David Grant Noble's *Ancient Ruins of the Southwest* and *Salinas*, edited by Noble, provide insight into the lives of New Mexico's early inhabitants. *Coronado: Knight of Pueblos and Plains* by Herbert E. Bolton introduces the Spanish era in New Mexico while Marc Simmons makes it personal with *Coronado's Land: Essays on Daily Life in Colonial New Mexico* and *The Last Conquistador: Juan de Oñate and the Settling of the Far Southwest*. The important role of the Catholic church in the state's history is covered in Paul Horgan's *Lamy of Santa Fe: His Life and Times*, Bishop Henry Granjon's memoir *Along the Rio Grande: A*

Pastoral Visit to Southwest New Mexico in 1902, and *Saints in the Valleys: Christian Sacred Images in the History, Life and Folk Art of Spanish New Mexico* by José E. Espinosa.

Several first-person accounts provide insight into the early Territorial period including those of W.W. H. Davis in *El Gringo: New Mexico and Her People*, Josiah Gregg's *Commerce of the Prairies*, and Susan Shelby Magoffin's *Down the Santa Fe Trail and Into Mexico*.

It is often difficult to separate the events of local history from their place in the state's history. Carole Larson's *Forgotten Frontier: The Story of Southeastern New Mexico* is really a history of the impact of Anglo settlement in that part of the state. *Gateway to Glorieta: A History of Las Vegas, New Mexico* by Lynn Perrigo is as much a history of the Santa Fe Trail as it is of Las Vegas. *Albuquerque* by Marc Simmons is the story of New Mexico's coming of age.

On the other hand, *Aztec: A Story of Old Aztec from the Anasazi to Statehood* by C.V. Koogler and Virginia Koogler Whitney, *Pioneers of the Mesilla Valley* by Paxton Price, and *Madrid Revisited; Life and Labor in a New Mexico Mining Camp in the Years of the Great Depression* by Richard Melzer, *Ruidoso Country* by Frank Mangan, and *Greetings from Gallup: Six Decades of Route 66* by Sally Noe are specific to their place in time. Local histories such as *Do You Remember Luna? 100 years of Pioneer History, 1883-1983*, *The History of Luna County*, and *Treasurers of History II: Chaves County Vignettes*, edited by Elvis B. Fleming and Ernestine Chesser Williams are histories recalled by those whose families settled the area.

Several books cover topics of specific interest to the state's history. Halka Chronic's *Roadside Geology of New Mexico* is a valuable, well-written reference as is Ira G. Clark's *Water in New Mexico*. *New Mexico Women: Intercultural Perspectives*, edited by Joan M. Jensen and Darlis A Miller is an important contribution to women's history. *New Mexico's Railroads: A Historical Survey* by David F. Myrick and *Railroads and Railroad Towns of New Mexico*, edited by Ree Sheck, and *The Harvey Girls: Women who Opened the West* by Lesley Poling Kempes provide the broad view of New Mexico's railroad era. *Ghost Towns and Mining Camps of New Mexico* by James E. and Barbara Sherman is an illustrated guide to the mining era. Peggy Pond Church's *The House at Otowi Bridge* and *The Day the Sun Rose Twice* by Ferenc Morton Szasz best capture the human drama of Los Alamos during the making of the atomic bomb. *Doctors of Medicine in New Mexico: A History of Health and Medical Practice 1886-1986* by Jake W. Spidle, Jr. covers the importance of health seekers in New Mexico history.

New Mexico's cultural character is covered extensively in *The Lore of New Mexico* by Marta Weigle and Peter White. Arrell Morgan Gibson covers the era of the artist in *The Santa Fe and Taos Colonies: Age of the Muses, 1900-1942*, while Paul Horgan's *Peter Hurd: A Portrait Sketch from Life* profiles one of the state's favorite painters. Richard W. Etulain's *Re-Imagining the Modern American West: A Century of Fiction, History and Art* provides a contemporary cultural overview. The essays in *Contemporary New Mexico, 1940-1990*, edited by Etulain, cover the often overlooked post-war period.

Finally, articles in *New Mexico Magazine* and the *New Mexico Historical Review* provide an on-going chronicle of the state's cultural and historical heritage.

Index

HOUSES in TIME

Designed by J. McKinzie
Text set in Palatino
Display set in Papyrus
Printed on 120 GSM Matte Art stock